Emma Lazarus   *Courtesy Library of Congress*

Emma Lazarus
Rediscovered

Eve Merriam

Introduction and Afterword by
Morris U. Schappes

Biblio Press
New York

This is an authorized reprint of *Emma Lazarus:Woman With A Torch*, by Eve Merriam, published by the Citadel Press, New York, 1956 by arrangement with Carol Publishing Group, Secaucus, NJ, 1998.

Permission to quote from this edition, *Emma Lazarus Rediscovered* can only be granted by the Publisher, Biblio Press, POB 20195, London Terrace Station, New York, NY 10011.

Library of Congress Cataloging-in-Publication Data

Merriam, Eve. 1916-
　　[Emma Lazarus, woman with a torch]
　　Emma Lazarus rediscovered / Eve Merriam : introduction
by Morris U. Schappes.
　　　　p.　　cm.
　　Originally published: Emma Lazarus, woman with a torch, New York :
Citadel Press. 1956. With new Introd.
　　Includes bibliographical references (p.　　) and index.
　　Summary: A biography of this American poet, activist for human
causes, and friend to immigrants, who write the words now inscribed
on the Statue of Liberty.
　　ISBN 0-930395-28-X (pbk.) -- ISBN 0-930395-29-8 (lib. ed.).
　　1. Lazarus, Emma. 1849-1887.　2. Women poets, American--19th
century--Biography.　3. Women social reformers--United States-
-Biography.　4. Zionists--United States-Biography.　5. Jews--United
States-Biography.　[1. Lazarus, Emma. 1849-1887.　2. Poets.
American.　3. Jews--Biography.　4. Women--Biography.]　I. Title.
PS2234.M42　　1998
811'.4--dc21
　　[b]　　　　　　　　　　　　　　　　　　　　　　98-49679
　　　　　　　　　　　　　　　　　　　　　　　　　　　　CIP
　　　　　　　　　　　　　　　　　　　　　　　　　　　　AC

TO THE EVER GREEN MEMORY OF

MY MOTHER

Editor's Note

In the last chapter of this biography of Emma Lazarus, the author Eve Merriam cites the brief publishing history (by 1956) of works about or by Lazarus. She laments the paucity of available publications of her poems and "polemical pieces". She wonders about the "neglect", when Lazarus "had so much to say to her own age and to our own."

We have therefore added to this edition an Introduction and an Afterword by Morris U. Schappes (written in 1982) which greatly expands the subject of Emma Lazarus and her relationship to Jewish life, as well as her work as poet, translator and essayist.

The reader should also note the addition of a brief bibliography to this reprinted edition, indicating several citations about Lazarus between 1995 and the present.

CONTENTS

INTRODUCTION

There is only one reason why people should rediscover the life and work of Emma Lazarus today, but that is reason enough: she can still delight, stir, inspire and instruct.

Her sonnet, "The New Colossus," placed in 1903 on a plaque affixed to the Statue of Liberty, is known to millions, many of whom however do not even know that she wrote it. Of those who do, too few know that she wrote anything else. Yet that sonnet comes out of a profound and intense experience that was itself one part and one expression of something broader and richer.

For many years her writings have been practically inaccessible to the general public. The two volumes of her poetry, collected and published posthumously in 1889, have long been out of print and are virtually out of the market. Her prose was buried away in the brittle, yellow pages of magazines of the 1880's.

This little selection,* which having compiled I now contemplate with chagrin because of all the valuable material I have been compelled to omit, is a beginning not only toward the rehabilitation of a needlessly dusty reputation. It is also, I believe, a contribution to the present intellectual and emotional life both of American Jews and of non-Jews here and abroad. Some day, and I hope it is soon, there may be a complete collection of her poetry and prose, including her letters, published in a more sumptuous edition.[1] but it is in the spirit of Emma Lazarus herself that the present selection is issued in this form, now, without more delay. When, in 1882, Emma Lazarus was urging *The American Hebrew* to publish her *Songs of a Semite*, she wrote to the magazine: "It is my idea to have the pamphlet issued at as low a price and in as simple a form as possible." Eager then for a popular audience, she saw to it that the paper-covered edition sold for twenty-five cents. Only two or three years before that she had, with modest objectivity, written to Edmund Clarence Stedman, the literary critic and editor, lamenting that she had "accomplished nothing to stir, nothing to awaken, to teach or to suggest, nothing that the world could not equal-

---

*The above is the original Introduction by Morris U. Schappes in the 1982 edition of *Emma Lazarus, Selections from Her Poetry & Prose,* published by the Emma Lazarus Federation of Women's Clubs, NY.
[1]See Schappes references at end of this introduction.

ly well do without." But by 1882, having been so deeply stirred herself, she was awakening others; and she was driven to seek as wide an audience as possible. Our judgment today must be "that the world could not equally well do without" the work of Emma Lazarus.

Born in New York on July 22, 1849, Emma Lazarus was brought up in the wealthy and fashionable home of her father, Moses, who was in the sugar refining industry until his retirement in 1865 at the age of fifty-two. Her great-grandparents (Samuel Lazarus on her father's side and Simon Nathan on her mother's) had been in this country at the time of the American Revolution. Her parentage was both Ashkenazic and Sephardic.

Shy and sensitive, she always clung closely to a family circle that was knit in intimacy with unusual tightness. Emma's education was wholly with private tutors, who apparently encouraged her to master foreign languages that were to extend her horizons. Thus when, in her seventeenth year, her first collection is published under the title, *Poems and Translations,* it includes translations from Hugo, Dumas, Schiller, and Heine. In 1871, when *Admetus and Other Poems* appears, she reveals a command of Italian in her translation of Leopardi, continues to translate Heine, and adds Goethe to her list. Later she was to translate from Petrarch and Alfred de Musset; and in the last years of her tragically short life she studied Hebrew in order to be able to translate from the Hebrew poets of medieval Spain without the intermediary of the German versions of these poets she had formerly used.

From the beginning, also, some of her interests were topical, to the extent at least that the Civil War and its aftermath penetrated to her comparatively sheltered existence and stimulated her to poetic compositions of unexpected dignity in one so young. Nevertheless, even after her second book had been issued and favorably received both in England and here, Thomas Wentworth Higginson, abolitionist distinguished especially for his command of a Negro regiment in the Civil war and an outstanding man of letters, wrote to his sisters from Newport in 1872, after making Emma's acquaintance: "...She is rather an interesting person...she has never seen an author till lately, though she has corresponded with Emerson. It is curious to see how mentally famished a person may be in the very best society."

It was not to be many years before authors and other men of affairs were to be speaking of her in different terms. That she was handsome, her pictures demonstrate. But she was to prove intelligent far beyond the expectations even of men gallant and liberal enough to concede that women might have brains. To a growing circle she was to show that, in certain circumstances, the tepid grace of "femininity" could combine with intellectual strength to produce a character both ardent and firm. But I am anticipating my account...

If fashionable society could not adequately nourish an Emma Lazarus, books did, and in Emerson's view, somewhat too exclusively. Emerson already in his mid-sixties, was not too old to recognize a fresh and youthful talent in her first volume in 1866, especially when he found such a note of earnestness in it. Corresponding with her in 1868 and 1869, he encouraged her and helped directly to shape her mind. He suggested she read Marcus Antoninus, the Bhagavad-Gita,[2] and Thoreau and Walt Whitman, but most of all Shakespeare for economy and effectiveness of rhetoric. She had sent him *Admetus*, which he hailed as "a noble poem," an opinion in which he was not shaken even when William Dean Howells, the country's outstanding novelist and editor, rejected it for publication in *The Atlantic Monthly*.

Emerson guided her to a process of condensation that improved the work. Yet he acutely put his finger on a major problem in the development of Emma Lazarus when he wrote to her on January 20, 1869: "...I do not know but the sole advice I have to offer is a pounding on the old string, namely, that though you can throw yourself so heartily into the old world of Memory, the high success must ever be to penetrate into & show the celestial element in the despised Present, & detect the deity that still challenges you under all the gross and vulgar masks." In her maturity Emma Lazarus was to write movingly of the Present, but she was to grow in such a way that even when she wrote of Yesterday it was because that particular Past was timely and a signpost to Tomorrow.

In 1876 when she visited for a wonderful week with Emerson at his home, she left for him the proof-sheets of *The Spagnoletto*, a five act verse tragedy with the scene laid in Italy in 1655. Emma insisted on publishing it only, however, for "private circulation." Three or four years later she composed the powerful drama, *The Dance to Death*, a story of the persecution of the Jews in Thuringia (Germany) in 1349. For several years she kept it unpublished, but when events in Europe proclaimed the utter timeliness of it, she published it serially in *The American Hebrew*, from June 30 to September 1, 1882, and then made it the main work in her proudly titled pamphlet, *Songs of a Semite*. The two subjects, her treatment of them, and her own attitude to them are landmarks in the growth of Emma Lazarus.

After the cordial reception accorded *Admetus and Other Poems* in 1871, she turned her hand to a prose romance based on an incident in Goethe's life, published in 1874 as *Alide*. She sent a copy to Turgenev, then in France, whose work, which she read in translation, had so much impressed her, and received in reply a very warm commendation, dated September 2, 1874: "...I am truly glad to say that I have read your book with the liveliest interest: It is very sin-

---

[2]Sanskrit poem of the Hindu devotional book.

cere and very poetical at the same time, the life and spirit of Germany have no secret for you—and your characters are drawn with a pencil as delicate as it is strong—I feel very proud of the approbation you give to my works—and of the influence you kindly attribute to them on your own talent: an author, who writes as you do—is not a 'pupil in art' any more, he is not far from being himself a master." Even generous words from such a source, however, did not lead Emma Lazarus to continue to write narrative prose. In fact she published little prose until 1881, when her biographical sketch of Heine appeared as an introduction to her volume of translations of his poems. When she used prose again, it was chiefly that of controversy and exhortation used in the defense of her people.

Most of those who have written about Emma Lazarus, both in her own time and more recently, have fallen prey to a confusing exaggeration. To dramatize a point that has its own sufficient drama, they have resorted to melodrama. They would have us believe that until Russian pogroms of the 1880's she had no interest in Jews or the problems of Jews, that she had virtually no consciousnesses of being a Jew. Evidence to the contrary is neglected or explained away.

The source of this needlessly strained interpretation is probably the biographical sketch included in the edition of her poems published in 1889, a sketch written by her own sister, Josephine. Therein we are told, for instance, that in 1881, when Emma Lazarus wrote the essay on Heine for her volume of translations, "she is as yet unaware or only vaguely conscious of the real bond between them," the fact that they were both Jewish. The reader is invited to judge for oneself from the excerpts given within. Again, the fact that in *The Century* of April 1882 there appeared her article, "Was the Earl of Beaconsfield {Disraeli] a Representative Jew?" is taken to signify that even then Judaism was "a dead letter to her...Nor had she any great enthusiasm for her own people." We are informed that "by a curious, almost fateful juxtaposition" the same issue of *The Century* carried an anti-Semitic defense of the Russian pogroms, and that is was in reaction to this article, to which Emma Lazarus replied most vigorously, that she suddenly found herself to be Jewish.[3]

Now it is true that the events in Russia and Madame Z. Ragozin's apology for them evoked a qualitative change in Emma Lazarus' consciousness of and activity in behalf of the Jews. But it will help us understand and appreciate the full significance of this change if we do not ignore the existing elements without which that change could not have taken place.

The record as I read it, however, shows that a Jewish consciousness was present in Emma Lazarus from her earliest days as a young writer. There is her

---

[3]See the Afterword for a discussion of the evidence for this issue.

poem, written at the age of eighteen, "In the Jewish Synagogue of Newport," published in her volume, *Admetus and Other Poems,* and immediately reprinted in *The Jewish Messenger.* There is her life-long interest in Heine, whose position as a Jew she so thoroughly understood and so brilliantly analyzed. There are are her translations from Gabirol and Halevy, published in *The Jewish Messenger* early in 1879. There is the aid she gave Dr. Gustav Gottheil of Temple Emanu-El "for some years before 1882" in his work on a collection of hymns and anthems adapted for Jewish worship. And, perhaps most significant, there is the fact that she wrote her profoundly moving play, *The Dance to Death,* a "few years" before it was published in 1882.

Then what was the character of the transformation that Emma Lazarus experienced? It was not from no interest in Jewry or a lack of interest to a sudden espousal of the cause of the Jew. Consciousness and interest there had always been, but it was an interest in Jewry distant and past, not present and American. The nature of the American Jewish community, however, must be remembered. In 1848, the year before her birth, there were only about 50,000 Jews in the entire country (out of a total population of about 23,000,000). By 1880, the number of Jews had increased to over 300,000, with the population as a whole having grown to more than 50,000,000. The social composition of this American Jewry had become largely middle-class; the majority were native born. There was an absence of those Jewish working class *masses* that we knew recently and that did not in fact begin to come into our country in great numbers until the very pogroms of the 1880's drove them out of Russia and East-Central Europe.

In such a context, her interest in Jewry was extensive but placid. She felt herself confronted with no *problems* that she and other Jews had to solve. No action was required. The persecuted Jews of fourteenth century Germany, whose condition and courage she dramatized in *The Dance to Death,* were long dead, and conditions in Germany had been changed. In general the extension of democracy was easing the burden of the Jew. Her sympathies were all with the oppressed, whose history she was reading, but it was a passive sympathy because she saw no present issue.

A change was presented to the world and to Emma Lazarus by the Russian pogroms that began in 1879 and increased in extent and ferocity during the next years. The pogroms evoked a passionate reaction she had not known before, and led her into active struggle against the brutalities abroad that her imagination rendered so vivid and her conscience made so personal. Now there was work to be done, refugees to be cared for, American Jews to be aroused to participation in the defense of a kin they were slow to recognize—too slow at least to suit Emma Lazarus. To enrich and to make more effective this new activity of hers, literary and otherwise, she found it necessary to enlarge and intensify her studies in Jewish history. Such was the new pattern of her life, fashioned out of old elements, but fired in the furnace of zealous activity.

Having access, because of her previous work, to non-Jewish magazines of distinction, she carried the intellectual struggle into these organs, publishing some of her most stirring prose and poetry in periodicals like *The Century* and *The Critic*. But while she battled the anti-Semitic enemy with one hand in these publications, she was using the other to arouse American Jewry itself to her own heightened sense of responsibility and fraternity. *The American Hebrew* grew in stature as she became for several years a regular contributor of drama, poetry, and prose. She developed a passion for Jewish history, but not for theology. Her concern was not so much with the articles of Jewish faith as with the plight of the Jewish people. She rewrote in prose and sang in poetry the vital lessons that could solve the problems of the Jews of the 1880's. The heroes, scholars and poets of the Jewish people—Bar Kochba and Rashi, Gabirol and Halevy—she made more than ever her own, and shared them with her people.

To Jew and non-Jew she presented with eloquence her concept of, and findings about, the Jews. The Jews loved life and nature. The Jews were thinkers whose thoughts had influenced both the Christian and Mohammedan world. The Jews were tough-fibered and resistant; oppression could bend but not break them, scatter them but not destroy. Jews were an able and resourceful people; they tended to excel in whatever pursuits were open to them.

The Jews needed and loved freedom. She wrote: "Until were are all free, we are none of us free." She wrote again: "Today, wherever we are free, are at home." Jews sought learning first, and wealth only secondarily, and that generally when they felt wealth was their only protection against insult. Their banner bore the democratic word Justice rather than the condescending or sentimental word Charity. Jews were rebels, not dogmatists. "The Jew (I say it proudly rather than deprecatingly) is a born rebel. He is endowed with a shrewd, logical mind, in order that he may examine and protest; with a stout and fervent heart, in order that the instinct of liberty may grow into a consuming passion, whereby, if need be, all other impelling motives shall be swallowed up." Jews would follow the truth, therefore, wherever it led, despite the fact that for the Jew it so often led to persecution. Maybe others—non-Jews—also shared these ideals. But the non-Jews were the *dominant* Christians and could have applied their principles—yet so often did not. These things she learned and these she taught in words noble and stark.

To whom did she speak them? She looked about her. American Jewry seemed to her comfortable, self-centered, indifferent too often to the condition of Jews in undemocratic countries of Europe. What did they have in common, they thought, with the thin-faced, pale, Ghetto Jew, earlocks long, "the caftaned wretches" of East Europe? In words without malice but sharp and stinging she told the rich American Jew that his freedom depended on the state of the pogrom-ridden Jews of the Caucasus. The American Jews may have squirmed, but they heeded her, when she issued the challenge: where is the American Ezra who will lift the Banner of the Jew and use it as an international battle-standard? Perhaps some of them even reflected that the American Ezra might be named Emma.

She visited the Jewish immigrants arriving from Russia and huddled in refuges on Ward's Island. She studied them and their plight, these Jews who had, by law and terror, been kept out of so many of the productive pursuits of mankind. With Heine she noted that each country gets the Jews it deserves or the Jews that it makes (a theme that recurs; see "Raschi in Prague" and "Russian Christianity versus Modern Judaism"). What Jews would our country make, and get? In the United States the Jew was "the free citizen of a Republic." Several times she noted the fateful fact that 1492 was the year in which the Jews were driven from Spain while Columbus was discovering America to "bequeath a Continent to Freedom." (See "1492" and "By the Waters of Babylon.") The more conscious of her Jewishness Emma Lazarus became, the prouder she grew of America. She wrote: "We possess the double cosmopolitanism of the American and the Jew."

It is true she observed and felt the existence of anti-Semitism in the land. When an anti-Semitic article appeared in *The Sun*, the New York daily, she complained in a letter to Philip Cowen "that this contempt and hatred underlies the general tone of the community towards us, and yet when I even remotely hint at the fact that we   are not a favorite people I am accused of stirring up strife and setting barriers between the two sects..." She even knew a Jew who was alarmed whenever another Jew distinguished himself in any way because of the envy and antagonism such ability might arouse. But she would not be hushed.

For her America was to be free, its democracy to be thoroughly tested. American Jews, these new immigrants especially, must do everything—not only those few things allowed them in European despotisms—they must farm and work and build and trade and learn and create and teach. How she thrilled when her friend Michael Heilprin showed her a letter from a Russian immigrant settled in Texas, a farmer, happy, with pogroms only a memory and with democratic sun overhead (see "In Exile"). Manual training was needed. What Booker T. Washington was to preach to the Negro people she taught the Jews. They must conquer new forms of labor. Interest in her idea spread. She lived to see the founding of The Hebrew Technical Institute, of which she was acknowledged to be the original inspiration.

But how many Jews could come to this America? There must be other solutions. With democracy so limited in Europe—Czars, Kaisers, tyrants regnant so widely—Jews needed a home of their own, a state where they could become a nation again. George Eliot, to whom she dedicated *The Dance to Death*, had thought of it and had made her Daniel Deronda speak of it. Another English writer, Laurence Oliphant, traveling in Palestine, had repeated it. Emma Lazarus made the idea her own and began to discuss it with her special vigor in *The American Hebrew*. Her solution was not intended for American Jews, who, she made it clear, would, could, and should stay here. But the Russian Jew, the Polish, Rumanian, Hungarian—the oppressed and the haunted millions of Europe—they needed it. It was her answer to the lack of democracy on the Continent. Herzl's concept, to become known as Zionism, was still unheard of when she expressed her aspiration for the conditions of a normal national life for the Jews.

Furthermore, Emma Lazarus looked where it was forbidden and daring to look. In the Mosaic Code she found the ethics and foundation of the idea then so fresh—Socialism. She disputed with surprised Christians their claim to having originated Socialist ideals. The basis was in the Mosaic Code, she insisted. And wasn't Marx, weren't other leaders of the socialist movement, Jews? Proudly she claimed her own.

In England, there was a poet whom she had long admired, imitated, and emulated, William Morris. He was a Socialist, a Marxian. When she went to England in the spring of 1883, she made sure to seek him out, spending a day with him at his factory in Surrey, and wrote about it for *The Century* in July, 1886, after she had met him again on her second trip to England. Morris and Socialism were being misrepresented. In the article she set out to explain how good and sincere Morris was, how his poetry had led to his politics, and what his politics were. "The passion for beauty," she wrote of Morris and perhaps of herself too, "which unless balanced by a sound and earnest intelligence is apt to degenerate into sickly and selfish aestheticism, inflames him with a burning desire to bring all classes of humanity under its benign influence." Moses, Marx, and William Morris—she claimed them all.

If many, Jew and non-Jew, did not follow her in such sweep and boldness of thought, she did not press the point. If the Jews in America wrote and acted with full consciousness of their brethren in other lands, and also resisted the manifestations of anti-Semitism even here, her avowed mission would be accomplished. In London she had been received "with great distinction" by prominent Jewish leaders, some of whom were converted to advocacy of her views on a Jewish national state. Non-Jews in literary and social circles had also honored her as poet and Jew. She returned refreshed and inspirited in the fall of 1883, taking again to her writing and public work. But within the year personal calamity overtook her. In August 1884 she became ill. On March 9, 1885 the father she loved so dearly died, and the blow was heavy. In May she went again to Europe, stayed more than two years, visited England, then The Hague, Paris, Pisa, Florence, Rome, while all the time the fatal cancer devastated her. She could not help comparing herself to Heine, similarly racked with illness and dying by degrees on his "mattress-grave." But despite the wasting horror of the body, her mind was alert and reached out to new fields. To her devotion to music and the theater was now added a zest for serious study of painting;she left unfinished a work on the "genius and personality" of Rembrandt.

In December, 1883 she wrote, in the new form of the prose-poem, the last work she was to live to see published. "By the Waters of Babylon," in *The Century* in March 1887, is the beautiful summation of her character and ideals, and of her most mature style. In 1880, in the poem, "Echoes," Emma Lazarus expressed the feeling that she was handicapped because she was a woman and alone. "Late-born and woman-souled," she was "one in love with solitude and song." She dared not "cope...with the world's strong-armed warriors." Not hers to "recite the dangers, wounds, and triumphs of the fight." She thought then she was one "who veiled and screened by womanhood must grope." But in the last five or six years of her life she strode from solitude into a fighting fraternity with her people that made her a leader of Jews on two continents and of the American people as a whole too. These words of Liebhaid von Orb's in *The Dance to Death* have a poignancy beyond that of the drama itself.

> *God help me! Shall my heart crack for love's loss*
> *That meekly bears my people's martyrdom?*
> *He lives—I feel it—to live or die with me.*
> *I love him as my soul—no more of that.*
> *I am all Israel's now—til this cloud pass,*
> *I have no thought, no passion, no desire,*
> *Save for my people.*

Having imaginatively written these words a few years before 1882, she lived them fully after that year.

When she returned from Europe to New York on July 31, 1887 she was grievously ill. She died on November 19, 1887, and was buried in the family lot at Beth Olam, Cypress Hills, N.Y.

Emma Lazarus was widely mourned. She was more than a literary figure. From London, Robert Browning cabled to *The American Hebrew* that he "associates himself with the admiration for the genius and love of the character of his lamented friend..." John G. Whittier, the venerable warrior and poet, wrote: "Since Miriam sang of deliverance and triumph by the Red Sea, the Semitic race has had no braver singer. 'The Crowing of the Red Cock,' written when the Russian sky was red with blazing Hebrew homes is an indignant and forceful lyric worthy of the Maccabean age. Her 'Banner of the Jew,' has the ring of Israel's war trumpets." The Southern writer, George W. Cable, expressed perhaps the conscience she had stimulated among non-Jews when he declared: "...she was the worthy daughter of a race to which the Christian world owes a larger debt of gratitude, incurred from the days of Abraham until now, and from which it should ask more forgiveness than to and from any other people that ever trod the earth."

There were similar statements in the Memorial Number of *The American Hebrew*, December 9, 1887, and in a later issue, October 5, 1888, from Claude G. Montefiore in London, from Edmund C. Stedman, from Edward Eggleston, preacher, historian, and Hoosier Schoolmaster, from Professor Hjalmar H. Boyesen of Columbia University, from John Hay, novelist, biographer of Lincoln, and Secretary of State, from E.L. Godkin of the *Poet* and Dana of the *Sun*, from Harriet Beecher Stowe and Thomas Wentworth Higginson; from poets, critics, and leaders of the Jewish community.

In her youth, Emerson had directed her to the reading of Walt Whitman, the great poet of our democracy. After her death, Whitman said to Horace Traubel one day: "She must have had a great, sweet, unusual nature."

Her name and her sonnet are fittingly wrought in metal in the pedestal of the Statue of Liberty. When America needed a poet to express what America meant to the world and to Americans, it turned to Emma Lazarus. As more Americans, Jewish and non-Jewish, come to know more of her work, she will resume a place in their hearts and minds that still needs to be filled. She led us briefly while she lived, and her thoughts led us for a time after she died. But there is more in Emma Lazarus than is remembered. We need that more.

Morris U. Schappes

REFERENCES

See my own collection: *The Letters of Emma Lazarus,* 1868-1885, New York Public Library publication, 1949.

The first biography of Lazarus in 1949, was by H.E. Jacob, *The World of Emma Lazarus.* (See my critical review in *American Literature,* January, 1950.)

Another biography, *Emma Lazarus* by Dan Vogel, Twayne Publishers, Boston, United States Authors Series, 1981, was reviewed by me in *Jewish Currents Magazine,* NYC, December, 1981.

Editor's note: See Bibliography at end of this book for some recent writings on Lazarus.

Morris U. Schappes

Long an expert in the field of American Jewish history, Morris U. Schappes, formerly of the English Department of the City College of New York (1928-1941), is the editor of *Selections from the Prose and Poetry of Emma Lazarus* and *The Letters of Emma Lazarus, 1868-1885,* published by the New York Public Library in 1949.

He has contributed articles and reviews to publications of the *American Jewish Historical Society, Minnesota History, New York History, American Literature,* the *Modern Language Association, Jewish Life, Chicago Jewish Forum,* and other journals.

Since 1958 he has been the editor of *Jewish Currents,* a monthly. In 1950 his monumental work, *A Documentary History of the Jews in the U.S., 1654-1875,* was published by Citadel Press, with a third updated edition in 1971 from Schocken Books.

Widely appreciated for his achievement as writer, editor and scholar, his peak was attained on his 90th birthday in 1997 when he was honored at the *Jewish Currents* annual dinner. Then, the President of the Borough of Manhattan came personally to present to him and the cheering audience, a Proclamation "...in recognition of this inspiring thinker and doer," naming the date as "Morris U. Schappes Day."

1

THE HOUSE WITH FINE CURTAINS

❦ The wealth of Manhattan, in the mid-Eighteen Hundreds, was shared by two distinct groups. There were the new-rich "Avenoodlers" with their recently built mansions on Fifth Avenue, showy and glittering. There were also the more modest brownstone dwellers, whose wealth had accreted over the generations.

The family of Emma Lazarus belonged to the latter. They lived in a tastefully (and expensively) furnished house in the fashionable Union Square section of the city: at number 36 West Fourteenth Street. Their residence was convenient to the theatre, to the opera, to the shopping district. Their carpets were heavy, their curtains and teacups fine, their windows often closed to the clanging, horse-drawn traffic out in the streets.

For the streets were very noisy. Manhattan had become a half-million-populated island. At Broadway and Fulton Street, at any hour of the day, you could see vast crowds gathering on the "shilling side" (east, where the cheaper merchandise was offered for sale) or on the "dollar side" (west, where the shops displayed more expensive goods). Crowds collected there merely to attempt a crossing from one side of the street to the other. And it was not unusual for the crossing to take half an hour—so teeming was the traffic with hackney-coaches, omnibuses, carriages, bustled and booted pedestrians.

At A. T. Stewart's famous emporium, there were costly cashmere shawls and glistening emeralds imported from the Orient. On the docks, in construction gangs, and in the work-

shops, were immigrant laborers from all Europe—led to New
York by the jewel of hope.

There was talk of paving the streets as far north as Twenty-
third. There was talk of P. T. Barnum's latest sensation—Jenny
Lind, singing at Castle Garden, and netting more than twelve
thousand dollars for a single concert, at a time when a dollar
had the value of ten today.

There was talk of another hall filled to overflowing: the
Broadway Tabernacle, where a Women's Rights convention
lasted for two days, brought delegates from as far away as Chicago. There was literary talk of Whittier, Emerson, Melville.

Yes, gold might have been discovered recently on Captain
Sutter's farm in California, but—as always—there was no place
like New York.

The family of Emma Lazarus had lived in New York for
many generations. Her parents and grandparents were all New
Yorkers born and bred. One of her great-grandparents was a
Sephardic Jew from Portugal, who had fled the Spanish Inquisi-
tion and emigrated to London and then the West Indies.

Moses Lazarus, Emma's father, became one of New York's
solidly wealthy citizens. The sign of his fortune could be seen
on family tables, for his business was sugar refining. His social
success could be seen in other activities. He was a founder of the
Knickerbocker Club and belonged to the historic Shearith Israel
Congregation. (The family as a group belonged to one of the
most affluent and influential congregations—the Spanish- Portuguese Synagogue.)

Moses' wife suited his station in life. In 1840, he had married
Esther Nathan, daughter of a Jewish family in New York as
prominent as the Lazaruses themselves. Esther's brother Benjamin, for example, was elected a member of the powerful New
York Stock Exchange, and a director of the Chicago and North-
western Railroad. Other members of the Nathan family were
distinguished in the legal profession. On the Nathan side of her

family, Emma was a first cousin to Supreme Court Justice Benjamin Cardozo.

Esther Nathan Lazarus became a devoted wife, attentive mother. After the initial tragedy of a male child stillborn, it seemed there would never be a son to inherit the Lazarus name and fortune.

A trio of girls came along in the next six years—Sarah, Mary, and Josephine. Surely, after three females in a row, the next baby would be a boy. Elijah they might call him, or Ezekiel. Perhaps Eliezer—in honor of Moses' father. Eliezer—yes, that would make a strong, masculine-sounding name.

On July 22, 1849, Eliezer turned out to be Emma. Dark-eyed, brown-haired, her features fine and at the same time boldly defined. With her thick cap of glossy curls, and hair growing like dark silken down along her ears, to edge her cheeks —what a beautiful baby boy she would have made . . .

In Jewish families of the time, boys were especially prized, and while the Lazaruses were not devout, Jewish mores were definitely a part of their life. Friday evening was the Sabbath Eve; and how could there be a real Passover Seder without a son to ask the Four Questions?

Perhaps a future poet in the family brings luck. At any rate, Eliezer Frank was born the following year. Then Agnes and Annie, and the family picture was rounded out. (Hope for another son was finally given up when, in 1856, a second male child died at birth.)

Since the Lazaruses were affluent, they could afford private tutors for their children. Emma had a gift for languages and learned French, Italian, and German readily. Her thirst for books could not be quenched. One by one she went through stories written for children, then the volumes in her father's imposing library.

Even when she relaxed from books, her play was literary.

Her dolls had names taken from the legends of King Arthur's Court, or from Greek and Roman mythology.

She may have dreamed of being a golden-haired princess or goddess, dwelling in a misty, ancient time when women were glorified. In her family she must have felt overshadowed. Her only brother (a year younger than she!) glowed among his sisters like a tiger lily in a field of common clover.

And among the six sisters she could not claim any distinction. She was not the beauty of the family; she was neither Sarah the eldest, nor Annie the baby.

More and more she lived in books, turned up a quiet face to the enormous adult world bustling about, reserved her thoughts for the fragmentary verses she was already beginning to jot down.

For the impulse to write poetry came when she was very young. Unlike many child prodigies, however, who skyrocket and then fizz out, the impulse strengthened and became a glowing force all her life.

Her sonnet "Echoes," written when she was only twenty-one, expresses her search for fulfilment. Scanned quickly, it seems romantic, a conventional, youthful lament.

> Late-born and woman-souled I dare not hope,
> The freshness of the elder lays, the might
> Of manly, modern passion shall alight
> Upon my Muse's lips, nor may I cope
> (Who veiled and screened by womanhood must grope)
> With the world's strong-armed warriors and recite
> The dangers, wounds, and triumphs of the fight;
> Twanging the full-stringed lyre through all its scope.
> But if thou ever in some lake-floored cave
> O'erbrowed by rocks, a wild voice wooed and heard,
> Answering at once from heaven and earth and wave,
> Lending elf-music to thy harshest word,
> Misprize thou not these echoes that belong
> To one in love with solitude and song.

Read it over again. "Late-born and woman-souled" . . . "veiled and screened." It is significant that she is conscious of the status of women and dares to voice it. And, although the poem claims that as a woman she cannot "cope with the world's strong-armed warriors" or twang "the full-stringed lyre through all its scope," we can be sure that she is not going to content herself with a half-string! No, although the last lines of the poem strike a minor chord, this is anything but a passive poem. It is not a sighing assumption of a secondary role in life; rather it is a calling out to be accepted as part of humankind. That call would be heard through all her work.

Books were not an escape to Emma; they were a corridor opening out into many rooms, with windows on the world. Language, literature was a living, breathing house with a working fireplace—smoke spiraled upward into the sky. And of all forms of literature, she chose poetry as the most direct, the most immediate, and the most emotional.

She was only eleven when the Civil War broke out in 1861. Lincoln immediately issued a call for volunteers to preserve the Union and in immediate response, the *Jewish Messenger* of New York printed an urgent editorial supporting the President's call. ". . . The time is past for forbearance and temporizing. We are now to *act*, and sure we are, that those whom these words may reach, will not be backward in realizing the duty that is incumbent upon them—to rally as one man for the *Union* and the *Constitution*. The Union—which binds together, by so many sacred ties, millions of freemen—which extends its hearty invitation to the oppressed of all nations, to come and be sheltered beneath its protecting wings—shall it be severed, destroyed, or even impaired? Shall those, whom we once called brethren, be permitted to overthrow the fabric reared by the noble patriots of the revolution, and cemented with their blood?

"And the Constitution—guaranteeing to all the free exercise of their religious opinions—extending to all liberty, justice, and equality—the pride of Americans, the admiration of the world —shall that Constitution be subverted, and anarchy usurp the place of a sound, safe, and stable government, deriving its authority from the consent of the American people?

"The voice of millions yet unborn, cries out, 'Forbid it, Heaven!' The voice of the American people declares, in tones not to be misunderstood, 'It shall not be!'

"Then stand by the flag!"

The battle had to be taken up. The slave-owners of the South could not be allowed to spread their poison of race supremacy, to turn back the forward industrial march of history. There were Copperhead elements in New York, but few in the Jewish community.

Emma saw uncles and male cousins, clad in Union blue, hurrying to the battlefront. She witnessed the desperately quick farewells, the weeks, months of waiting, growing into years. She heard the clamor of the draft riots in New York City, the crackle of flames as the Negro orphan asylum was set on fire. She watched the women at home binding up their grief with useful work: meeting together to sew uniforms, blankets, bandages. . . . She saw the uniforms return, stained, dusty; the blankets with bullet holes. She saw the bittersweet family reunions, knew of families for whom reunion never came.

So among her earliest poems are several on the subject of war. She wrote of the shadows that remain, even in the sunlight of war's ending. The majority of her poems, however, as one would expect at that age, are on romantic themes taken from mythology or moods of nature.

Melancholy, plaintiveness enter in—not at all unnatural in an adolescent. "On A Lock Of My Mother's Hair" expresses a fourteen-year-old's thoughts on growing old. "In Memoriam" speaks of the untimely death of a young friend. Also, calling on her skill with foreign languages, she began to translate French and German poets.

Diffidently, she passed her poems around the family circle. Her father, quite rich at the age of fifty-two, had retired from business in 1865, and was now at home, helping to instruct the growing children. He had always enjoyed reading and could claim acquaintance with men prominent in all the arts—literature, music, the theatre, painting.

He looked over her notebook. His daughter Emma had a real talent. Take the first stanza of this poem, for example, called forth by the war.

BREVET BRIGADIER-GENERAL FRED WINTHROP
(Written April 12, 1865)

More hearts will break than gladden when
The bitter struggle's past;
The giant form of Victory must
A giant's shadow cast.

"The giant form of Victory must a giant's shadow cast . . ." She was using language as a tool, not merely tasting words as one would sample a box of sweets. She dared to repeat the word "giant," thereby giving the verse a homeliness, a simplicity, and, yes, a strength. The rest of the stanzas, he noted, were not up to that high mark, yet even so. . . . The poem showed surprising maturity and compassion, coming from a teen-age girl.

He leafed through more pages. Quite an achievement: here were thirty original poems, and nearly a dozen excellent translations of Heine, Dumas, Hugo. His daughter should be encouraged. Why not have her manuscript printed? For private circulation only, of course—to show off to prideful cousins, uncles, doting aunts, close friends.

So, in 1866, H. O. Houghton and Company published a slim little volume: *Poems and Translations by Emma Lazarus. Written between the ages of fourteen and sixteen.*

The title page offered a witty epigram from Lebrun:

They have just stolen from me—how I pity thy grief!—
All my manuscript verse;—how I pity the thief!

And the dedication read simply: "To My Father."

Family and friends praised the book, and Emma herself must

have felt a warm stirring at the sight of her first work in print. (Many years later, she tried to destroy all copies of this earliest volume, which came to seem insignificant to her. Today only three copies are known.)

The reception of her book was enthusiastic enough so that the following year it was reprinted for general circulation. Ten new poems were added, one of them—"Remember"—on the theme of her Jewish ancestry.

Now Emma must have felt chilling doubt after the flush of her initial success. Family and friends could flutter over her work. Strangers would have a more objective attitude. And the critics—those peppery phrase-makers, what would they say?

Imagine her delight at hearing that the famous poet, William Cullen Bryant, had told a friend that her verses were "better than any I remember to have seen written by any American girl of eighteen."

Far greater delight was in store. One evening, her father escorted her to the house of the banker, Samuel Gray Ward. The living room was aglow with lights and literary talk.

Moses Lazarus walked over to an elderly man seated in an armchair, bowed to him in deference. "Sir, may I present my daughter?"

Emma looked down at the pattern of the carpet as she curtseyed, then looked up to gaze into the face of Mount Olympus itself. She was actually being presented to the Sage of Concord, to the great Ralph Waldo Emerson!

2

WORK IS A WOMAN

🌿 Emerson asked Emma to send a copy of her book to him at Concord. Returned there from his New York visit, he read and praised it. Far more important, he accepted Emma as a serious artist and offered constructive criticism. A correspondence took roots and prospered between the venerable master and the young girl on the threshold of a career. For all Emma's reverence for Emerson, her letters flowed freely, revealing her enthusiasms and interests, her concern with deepening her craft. Emerson, on his part treated her more like an equal than a novice.

"Go back and reread Shakespeare for economy of expression," he advised her. He also suggested that she could profit by turning to some contemporary figures, too—such as Thoreau and Whitman. At the same time, he cautioned her against leading too bookish a life. "Books are only tools," he insisted. "Books are a safe ground, and a long one, but still introductory only, for what we really seek is every comparison of experiences. To know if you have found therein what alone I prize, or still better, if you have found what I have never found—and yet is admirable to me also." It was a subject he liked to argue about. "Books so tyrannize over our solitude," he told her, "that we like to revenge ourselves by making them very secondary and merely convenient as hints and counters in conversations. . . . Yes, and I hold that we have never reached their best use until our own thought rises to such a pitch that we cannot afford to read much."

From the summer cottage where she was vacationing with her family, Emma wrote back: "I am dismissing printed books, not from any such high cause as you advise, but because I have a nobler, vaster, more suggestive book lying all around me, with leaves ever open, inviting me to study and admire and love." The woodland scene before her window showed a fine, sparkling day; the grass thick and luxurious, the trees ripe with fruit.

"I have only been reading Thoreau's Concord River and Letters," she continued, "and a poem or two of Walt Whitman —but these writers are so in harmony with Nature that they do not take me away from the scene."

Nature moved Emma deeply, and of the four seasons of the year, her favorite was the fall. Yet it was never for her "the dying fall," with leaves sere and withering. It was the triumphant, harvest time. She wrote to her mentor: "Of all seasons, Autumn is the one whose approach I love best to watch. I have seen with delight the bronzing trees of the woods, and the trembling poplars sprinkling their silver with gold, and the later flowers and fruits blooming and ripening."

Undoubtedly, there were already gestating within her the majestic songs she was to write of the Jewish New Year arriving at autumnal harvest time. For the consciousness of her Jewish heritage was already forming. She visited the historic synagogue at Newport, Rhode Island, and it is possible that she read and was stirred by the moving exchange of letters between George Washington and the members of the congregation.

The congregation wrote to welcome Washington to Newport in the summer of 1790:

"Deprived as we have hitherto been of the invaluable rights of free citizens, we now, (with a deep sense of gratitude to the Almighty Disposer of all events) behold a Government (erected by the Majesty of the People), a Government which to bigotry gives no sanction, to persecution no assistance—but generously affording to All liberty of conscience, and immunities of citizenship—deeming every one, of whatever nation, tongue, or language equal parts of the great governmental machine. This so ample and extensive federal union whose basis is Philanthropy, mutual confidence, and public virtue, we cannot but acknowledge to be the work of the Great God, Who ruleth in the armies of Heaven, and among the inhabitants of the Earth, doing whatsoever seemeth Him good.

"For all the blessings of civil and religious liberty which we enjoy under an equal and benign administration we desire to send up our thanks to the Ancient of days, the great Preserver of Men, beseeching Him that the Angel who conducted our forefathers through the wilderness into the promised land, may graciously conduct you through all the dangers and difficulties of this mortal life—and when like Joshua full of days, and full of honor, you are gathered to your Fathers, may you be admitted into the heavenly Paradise to partake of the water of life and the tree of immortality.

"Done and signed by order of the Hebrew Congregation in New Port, Rhode Island, August 17th, 1790."

Washington replied in the same spirit of rejoicing in a democratic government:

"The Citizens of the United States of America have a right to applaud themselves for having given to mankind examples of an enlarged and liberal policy, a policy worthy of imitation.

"All possess alike liberty of conscience and immunities of citizenship. It is now no more that toleration is spoken of, as if it was by the indulgence of one class of people, that another enjoyed the exercise of their inherent natural rights. For happily the government of the United States, which gives to bigotry no sanction, to persecution no assistance, requires only that they who live under its protection should demean themselves as good citizens, in giving it on all occasions their effectual support.

"It would be inconsistent with the frankness of my character not to avow that I am pleased with your favorable opinion of my administration, and fervent wishes for my felicity.

"May the children of the Stock of Abraham, who dwell in

this land, continue to merit and to enjoy the good will of the other inhabitants, while every one shall sit in safety under his own vine and fig-tree, and there shall be none to make him afraid.

"May the Father of all mercies scatter light and not darkness in our paths, and make us all in our several vocations useful here, and in His own due time and way everlastingly happy.

G. WASHINGTON"

In the famous shrine, Emma reflected upon the past, put her thoughts into a poem:

IN THE JEWISH SYNAGOGUE AT NEWPORT

Here, where the noises of the busy town,
The ocean's plunge and roar can enter not,
We stand and gaze around with tearful awe,
And muse upon the consecrated spot.

No signs of life are here: the very prayers
Inscribed around are in a language dead;
The light of the 'perpetual lamp' is spent
That an undying radiance was to shed.

This image of the "perpetual lamp" is to recur in her work many times. The lamp of light, of truth and justice: this was Emma's vision; but unlike many poets who become obsessed with a private symbolism, her meaning shone clear.

The poem continues:

What prayers were in this temple offered up,
Wrung from sad hearts that knew no joy on earth,
By these lone exiles of a thousand years,
From the fair sunrise land that gave them birth!

Again, an image of light in "the fair sunrise land that gave them birth." She is thinking of the ancient Jewish homeland in the East, where dawn begins. But the Jews were cast out from the sunrise land, forced to wander the earth in darkness. Now there is another light: the inspiration of America, of the New World welcoming them. From "this new world of light," she looks back upon the old:

Now as we gaze, in this new world of light,
Upon this relic of the days of old,
The present vanishes, and tropic bloom
And Eastern towns and temples we behold.

Again we see the patriarch with his flocks,
The purple seas, the hot blue sky o'erhead,
The slaves of Egypt,—omens, mysteries,—
Dark fleeing hosts by flaming angels led.

A wondrous light upon a sky-kissed mount,
A man who reads Jehovah's written law,
Midst blinding glory and effulgence rare,
Unto a people prone with reverent awe.

The pride of luxury's barbaric pomp,
In the rich court of royal Solomon—

The steady even beat of the lines has mounted to a crescendo.
She breaks off and returns to the earlier mood:

Alas! we wake; one scene alone remains,—
The exiles by the streams of Babylon.

Our softened voices send us back again
But mournful echoes through the empty hall;
Our footsteps have a strange unnatural sound,
And with unwonted gentleness they fall.

The weary ones, the sad, the suffering,
All found their comfort in the holy place,
And children's gladness and men's gratitude
Took voice and mingled in the chant of praise.

The funeral and the marriage, now, alas!
We know not which is sadder to recall;
For youth and happiness have followed age,
And green grass lieth gently over all.

Nathless the sacred shrine is holy yet,
With its lone floors where reverent feet once trod.
Take off your shoes as by the burning bush,
Before the mystery of death and God.

Classic themes, however, still absorbed her. She wrote "Admetus," a long, romantic poem with characters and scenes from Greek mythology. *Lippincott's,* the leading literary magazine of the day, printed it—as they did most of her poetry from this period on.

Emma dedicated the poem to Emerson. Her inscription could easily have been fulsome. "To my kind master, from his most humble servant" would not have been considered inappropriate, or even "To my lofty mentor, from his lowly apprentice." A young writer with less strength of character might well prefer such a relationship: that of pupil to teacher, of faltering youth being led by the strength and wisdom of age. That way, she could evade responsibility for her work by claiming immaturity. Or, if she chose, she could lean on the frailty of her sex in a male-dominated society. "To the great man, from his poor little poetess. . . ." Emma would have none of that. Her dedication read plainly: "To my friend, Ralph Waldo Emerson."

Emerson wrote that he regretted not meeting her again in person, so that he could learn more of her: "So had I been qualified for your ghostly counsellor in all emergencies, and at least might have had a basis for letters, and could never, as I may now, write wide of the mark."

Was this gallantry, or was he trying to break off their correspondence? Emma was forthright in her response: "I should like to tell you plainly and frankly my character and disposition, that you might guide and correct me, but it would be worse than uninteresting to you. And besides, I never believe such personal confessions are worth much, for there is always a certain vanity and egotism in thus holding up the glass to one's heart and mind. I think after all, modesty and the concealing of one's faults imply at least contrition and a desire to be better— but declaring them openly requires a degree of boldness and shamefacedness which tends to intensify them. And I know too beforehand, well enough that I never would confess the meanest or most contemptible, or if I did I would dignify them with some better name than they deserve, which would almost reconcile me to their possession. . . ."

She paused. She looked forward so to his letters, she would hate to have their correspondence brought to a halt. But she would not use tricks to continue it. Reluctantly, she concluded her letter to him: "So I am sorry to see that there is no forcing power to make friendship bud and blossom before years and experience have ripened it, and that I am forbidden to 'snatch at this slowest fruit in the whole garden of God.' "

And that was that: she would reveal herself in her work. Happily, the correspondence continued.

Admetus and Other Poems was published in 1871. The volume was received well in the United States and England—overpraised by several British critics who compared her to Browning, and even considered her in some ways his superior! Following the title poem dedicated to Emerson, there were three other romances in verse—"Orpheus," dedicated to her older sister Josephine; "Lohengrin," to her cousin Washington Nathan; and "Tannhäuser," to her mother.

The best of the book came at the last, with a number of strong, clear-calling lyrics. "Florence Nightingale" is a tribute to that famous nurse's work.

And in the series of poems entitled "Epochs," Emma expressed her conception of work:

> Yet life is not a vision nor a prayer,
> But stubborn work; she may not shun her task.
>
> But when she fills her days with duties done,
> Strange vigor comes, she is restored to health.
> New aims, new interests rise with each new sun,
> And life still holds for her unbounded wealth.
> All that seemed hard and toilsome now proves small,
> And naught may daunt her,—she hath strength for all.

Interestingly, the figure representing Work is a woman, not the conventional symbol of a man.

In this final section of the book, there are two more poems

that prove Emma's talent has already transcended her youth
and sheltered environment. "Heroes" deals not with the victory
achieved in battle by the Union soldier, but the far slower and
more difficult aftermath of war. It is a truly mature concept:

> . . . For brave dead soldiers, these:
> Blessings and tears of aching thankfulness,
> Soft flowers for the graves in wreaths enwove,
> The odorous lilac of dear memories,
> The heroic blossoms of the wilderness,
> And the rich rose of love.

> . . . But who has sung their praise,
> Not less illustrious, who are living yet? . . .

> . . . They who were brave to act,
> And rich enough their action to forget;
> Who, having filled their day with chivalry,
> Withdraw and keep their simpleness intact,
> And all unconscious add more lustre yet
> Unto their victory.

She summons up their daily lives as farmers, city workers:

> On the broad Western plains
> Their patriarchal life they live anew;
> Hunters as mighty as the men of old,
> Or harvesting the plenteous, yellow grains,
> Gathering ripe vintage of dusk bunches blue,
> Or working mines of gold;

> Or toiling in the town,
> Armed against hindrance, weariness, defeat,
> With dauntless purpose not to swerve or yield,
> And calm, defiant strength, they struggle on,
> As sturdy and as valiant in the street,
> As in the camp and field.

She thinks also of the wounded, the scarred veterans:

> And those condemned to live,
> Maimed, helpless, lingering still through suffering years,
> May they not envy now the restful sleep
> Of the dear fellow-martyrs they survive?
> Not o'er the dead, but over these, your tears,
> O brothers, ye may weep!

The unsung, those who live and work from day to day, these, finally, are the real heroes to Emma:

> New England fields I see,
> The lovely, cultured landscape, waving grain,
> Wide, haughty rivers, and pale, English skies.
> And lo! a farmer ploughing busily,
> Who lifts a swart face, looks upon the plain,—
> I see, in his frank eyes,
>
> The hero's soul appear.
> Thus in the common fields and streets they stand;
> The light that on the past and distant gleams,
> They cast upon the present and the near,
> With antique virtues from some mystic land,
> Of knightly deeds and dreams.

In "How Long?" she called upon her fellow writers to shake off the deadening weight of cultural influences of the Old World and turn for inspiration to the New:

> How long, and yet how long,
> Our leaders will we hail from over seas,
> Masters and kings from feudal monarchies,
> And mock their ancient song
> With echoes weak of foreign melodies?

She speaks out clearly: Stop imitating the English masters. The Revolutionary War was fought for freedom; why should we continue to tie ourselves culturally? America is a vast, broad world, not a cramping island. Different kinds of poetry, of music, of art must come forth here! So she contrasts England and America:

> That distant isle mist-wreathed,
> Mantled in unimaginable green,
> Too long hath been our mistress and our queen.
> Our fathers have bequeathed
> Too deep a love for her our hearts within.
>
> She made the whole world ring
> With the brave exploits of her children strong,
> And with the matchless music of her song.
> Too late, too late we cling
> To alien legends, and their strains prolong.

This fresh young world I see,
With heroes, cities, legends of her own;
With a new race of men, and overblown
By winds from sea to sea,
Decked with the majesty of every zone.

I see the glittering tops
Of snow-peaked mounts, the wid'ning vale's expanse,
Large prairies where free herds of horses prance,
Exhaustless wealth of crops,
In vast, magnificent extravagance.

She is like Walt Whitman in her patriotic exultation:

These grand, exuberant plains,
These stately rivers, each with many a mouth,
The exquisite beauty of the soft-aired south,
The boundless seas of grains,
Luxuriant forests' lush and splendid growth.

The distant siren-song
Of the green island in the eastern sea,
Is not the lay for this new chivalry.
It is not free and strong
To chant on prairies 'neath this brilliant sky.

The echo faints and fails;
It suiteth not, upon this western plain,
Our voice or spirit; we should stir again
The wilderness, and make the plain
Resound unto a yet unheard-of strain.

She was calling out to others, she was also calling to herself, of
course, to relinquish romantic visions of the past, of a way of
life different from the present reality. Even in the contemplation
of natural beauty it enters, as in these lines from a sonnet on
the forests and lakes of Maine:

. . . Eastward the sea, with its majestic plain,
Endless, of radiant, restless blue, superb
With might and music, whether storms perturb
Its reckless waves, or halcyon winds that reign,
Make it serene as wisdom. Storied Spain
Is the next coast, and yet we may not sigh

For lands beyond the inexorable main;
Our noble scenes have yet no history.
All subtler charms than those that feed the eye,
Our lives must give them; 'tis an aim austere,
But opes new vistas, and a pathway clear.

It is always easier to give advice than to take it, however poetically expressed. Emma still felt herself drawn by the romantic, the remote; and with many of her poems on classical themes praised so highly by the critics of America and England, it was hard for her to keep her gaze steadily on the here and now. It was hard to bear in mind all the time the advice Emerson had given her: that "I do not know but the sole advice I have to offer is a pounding on the old string, namely, that though you can throw yourself so heartily into the old world of Memory, the high success must ever be to penetrate into and show the celestial element in the despised Present, and detect the deity that still challenges you under all the gross and vulgar masks."

She had done some deft translating of scenes from Goethe's *Faust*. Now she began a rambling, romantic novel based on a love incident in the great German writer's life. *Alide* the novel was called, and Lippincott and Company published it in 1874. The book was dedicated to the associate editor of *Lippincott's* Magazine, Mrs. Lucy Hamilton Hooper, who had become Emma's close friend.

Alide was praised by no less a personage than Turgenev. "I am truly glad to say," he wrote to her, "that I have read your book with the liveliest interest: It is very sincere and very poetical at the same time; the life and spirit of Germany have no secret for you—and your characters are drawn with a pencil as delicate as it is strong. I feel very proud of the approbation you give to my works—and of the influence you kindly attribute to them on your own talent: an author, who writes as you do, is not a 'pupil in art' any more; he is not far from being himself a master."

These were remarks to cherish, for Turgenev's novels had affected Emma deeply. The ease with which he handled weighty ideas, the appreciative respect and understanding he showed for women: yes, her reading of Turgenev, she felt, must surely make its mark on her own work.

She saved his letter as a permanent treasure. It was well to keep his words before her now, on this cold December day, for a blow was about to fall.

Emerson had been compiling an anthology of what he considered the best contemporary poetry in the English-speaking world. The collection was issued by Emerson's Boston publishers, and the copy Emma ordered had just arrived.

We can imagine her mounting excitement. Quickly, she stripped off the outer wrapping. *Parnassus,* the shiny new title read. She was sure she had been given a place on that poetic peak.

Eagerly she scanned the list of almost two hundred authors. Here was Lucy Larcom, the New England poet who made her living as a factory hand; she deserved to be represented. And Julie Ward Howe, of course. There were also many minor women poets whose names Emma did not even recognize. But where was her own?

She went over the index more carefully. Not a line by Emma Lazarus.

She could scarcely believe it. Her first reaction was a numbing chill. She would close the book, she would freeze into immobility. She would not write another poem. She would remain silent.

But that was evasion. No, she would speak up now, while her wrath was great, before timidity set in. She would challenge the lord of Parnassus himself!

"36 West 14th St.

December 27th 1874

"My dear Mr. Emerson—

I cannot resist the impulse of expressing to you my extreme disappointment at finding you have so far modified the enthusiastic estimate you held of my literary labors as to refuse me a place in the large and miscellaneous collection of poems you have just published. I can only consider this omission a public retraction of all the flattering opinions and letters you have sent me, and I cannot in any degree reconcile it with your numerous expressions of extravagant admiration. . . ."

Why, oh why, she kept questioning herself. Why had he changed so?

"If I had either done anything to forfeit your friendship, or neglected the proper development and improvement of the gift you were pleased to rate so highly, I might partly account for the unexpected withdrawal of your interest in what I had already accomplished, but as I am innocent in both respects the fact remains as inexplicable as it is disappointing. . . ."

She paused, took a deep breath. She really must control her tone! But it was not the mighty man alone who had praised her work.

"Your favorable opinion having been confirmed by some of the best critics of England and America, I felt as if I had won for myself by my own efforts a place in any collection of American poets, and I find myself treated with absolute contempt in the very quarter where I had been encouraged to build my fondest hopes. This public neglect is in such direct variance with the opinions you have expressed to me in private, that it leaves me in utter bewilderment as to your real verdict. . . ."

That large sheaf of letters from him, tied up so carefully, preserved with such reverence! She took them out of her desk drawer.

"As you must have forgotten your own words, and to prove to you that my expectations were not unfounded, I will transcribe a few extracts from your letters, as it is the last time I can quote them. Of my poem 'Heroes,' you wrote 'Oh yes, the "Heroes" is good to write and read. The tone and sentiment of the poem are noble and the voice falters in reading it aloud.' When William Dean Howells refused 'Admetus' for the *Atlantic Monthly,* you said, 'Mr. Howells declines printing the poem and leaves us only the doubt whether he or we are in the wrong. I should have printed it thankfully and proudly; we must believe that his *Atlantic* portfolio is very rich in poetry, and I shall frankly own it if Sparta hath worthier daughters. You can well afford to receive back the fable but when will the *Atlantic* give me one as noble?' And after your first reading of 'Admetus,' you greeted me with an 'All hail!' saying, 'You have written a noble poem which I cannot enough praise. You have hid yourself from me till now, for the merits of the preceding poems did not unfold this fulness and high quality of power.' "

Emma put his letters down sadly. Should she keep them as a mockery, or destroy them? She returned them to their former resting place; when her head was not so throbbing, she would decide. Now she must finish her own words to him before her courage failed.

"I trust I may not be accused of arrogance in repeating such sentences as these, for I would have deemed it a wrong to yourself to have accepted them as anything less than the expression of a perfect sincerity. I frankly confess I never could have imagined that they were not sufficiently emphatic for your favorite poems, unless I had seen what panegyric you found for such as are worthy of a place in Parnassus.

"May I not now ask which alternative I am to adopt? Whether I must believe that the few years which have elapsed since you wrote me those letters have sufficed to make you reverse your opinion of my poems? Or whether that opinion was even then ill-considered, and expressed in stronger language than your critical judgment warranted?

"Begging that you will favor me with a reply at your earliest convenience, I remain

Very truly yours,

Emma Lazarus"

It was an extraordinary letter; it demanded an extraordinary answer.

3

OUT OF BOOKS INTO LIFE

❦ There was no answer at all.

Perhaps Emerson had expected Emma to maintain a polite, ladylike silence. By his own silence he may have wished to reproach her thus for speaking out of turn. Or, he may have been too angered by her letter to reply. It is barely possible that, from the lofty age of seventy-one, he was amusedly tolerant of this young woman of twenty-five. At any rate, Emma's letter went unanswered.

Had her relationship to him ever been one of hero-worship, of a schoolgirl "crush," as some critics have suggested, she might well have become embittered. But such was not the case.

That he had been a profound influence in her life there was no doubt. She could recall her former words about him now with a touch of irony: she had written of Emerson, "to how many thousand youthful hearts has not his word been the beacon—nay, more, the guiding-star that led them safely through periods of mental storm and struggle."

Well, now she would have to provide her own guiding star, her own light. So she continued to write, and her work improved. Perhaps she was spurred on by the idea of proving her worth to her former sponsor.

Lippincott's began to feature her poetry on a fairly regular basis.

Events of the day did not escape her. Reacting to the belated proposal to erect a monument to Byron, she poured scorn on the timid conservatism that had not dared to celebrate his living fame.

She took the newspaper headline for her title:

ON THE PROPOSAL TO ERECT A MONUMENT IN ENGLAND TO LORD BYRON

> *The grass of fifty Aprils hath waved green*
> *Above the spent heart, the Olympian head,*
> *The hands crost idly, the shut eyes unseen,*
>   *Unseeing, the locked lips whose song hath fled;*
> *Yet mystic-lived, like some rich, tropic flower,*
> *His fame puts forth fresh blossoms by the hour. . . ."*

Byron had gone to Greece, to help fight for independence;
he had met his death there, and the Greek patriots had honored
him—but not his native land of England.

> *An alien country mourned him as her son,*
>   *And hailed him hero: his sole, fitting tomb*
> *Were Theseus' temple or the Parthenon,*
>   *Fondly she deemed. His brethren bare him home,*
> *Their exiled glory, past the guarded gate*
> *Where England's Abbey shelters England's great.*
> *Afar he rests whose very name hath shed*
>   *New lustre on her with the song he sings.*
> *So Shakespeare rests who scorned to lie with kings,*
> *Sleeping at peace midst the unhonored dead.*
>
> *And fifty years suffice to overgrow*
>   *With gentle memories the foul weeds of hate*
> *That shamed his grave. The world begins to know*
>   *Her loss, and view with other eyes his fate . . .*

The image of the monument to be built in England now looms
up. The poem recalls Byron as he was, as he should be remembered, in all his humanity and courage, his daring to go beyond
the conventional:

> *Even as the cunning workman brings to pass*
> *The sculptor's thought from out the unwieldy mass*
> *Of shapeless marble, so Time lops away*
>   *The stony crust of falsehood that concealed*
>   *His just proportions, and, at last revealed,*
> *The statue issues to the light of day,*
>
> *Most beautiful, most human. Let them fling*
>   *The first stone who are tempted even as he,*

> And have not swerved. When did that rare soul sing
>   The victim's shame, the tyrant's eulogy,
>   The great belittle, or exalt the small,
>   Or grudge his gift, his blood, to disenthrall
>   The slaves of tyranny or ignorance?

Yes, Byron may have been unconventional in his personal
life, but that was a matter for petty scandal-mongers. What
mattered was his achievement, and that was truly great. Emma
concludes:

> The years' thick, clinging curtains backward pull,
> And show him as he is, crowned with bright beams . . .

She quotes from the drama of Cain: "Beauteous, and yet not
all as beautiful as he hath been or might be; Sorrow seems half
of his immortality."

>   . . . He needs
> No monument whose name and songs and deeds
> Are graven in all foreign hearts; but she
>   His mother, England, slow and last to wake,
>   Needs raise the votive shaft for her fame's sake:
> Hers is the shame if such forgotten be!

There was an anger, a passionate wrath arising in Emma's
work. She needed this core of new strength, for tragedy entered
her life. Early in 1876, her mother died. The close-knit family
circle was jaggedly broken.

Emma's poem, "A March Violet," suggests the sorrow of the
event and the slowly gathering after-strength acknowledging
that life goes on. For the verses take note of the wintry atmosphere still pervading the wooded spot where the poet stands.
Although the air is chilly and damp, already there are signs of
spring. Muted, shy in its color—still, the first March violet is a
token of new life, future warmth.

Lippincott's printed the poem and a few weeks later printed
another, longer poem dealing more directly with her feelings
about her mother, about all mothers. "La Madonna Della
Sedia" it is called, from Raphael's famous painting. The poem,
in dialogue form attempts to reveal the story behind the paint-

ing. Raphael is shown speaking with a mother nursing her baby. He is impressed with the dignity of her bearing, the glory of her role. He determines to paint her picture to capture for a later time:

> . . . the lights, the tints, the golden atmosphere,
> The genius of the scene—the mother-love.

In still another poem, Emma writes with reverence and joy of mothers throughout history. The Latin title "Mater Amabilis" (Loving Mother) suggests the endurance and continuity of the emotion from ancient times to all future times. And the structure, with its lulling, repeated beat of short lines alternating with long, shows her growing mastery of her craft. Form and content blend richly as the lines themselves move to a cradle-rocking cadence, to and fro, to and fro . . .

> Down the goldenest of streams,
>   Tide of dreams,
> The fair cradled man-child drifts;
> Sways with cadenced motion slow,
>   To and fro,
> As the mother-foot poised lightly, falls and lifts.
>
> He, the firstling,—he, the light
>   Of her sight,—
> He, the breathing pledge of love,
> 'Neath the holy passion lies,
>   Of her eyes,—
> Smiles to feel the warm, life-giving ray above.

The poem proceeds, expressing the mother's hopes and dreams for her son's future:

> She believes that in his vision,
>   Skies Elysian
> O'er an angel-people shine.
> Back to gardens of delight,
>   Taking flight,
> His auroral spirit basks in dreams divine.

Will the future be as radiant as she hopes? The dream mingles with reality:

But she smiles through anxious tears;
Unborn years
Pressing forward she perceives.
Shadowy muffled shapes, they come
Deaf and dumb,
Bringing what? dry chaff and tares, or full-eared sheaves?

What for him shall she invoke?
Shall the oak
Bind the man's triumphant brow?
Shall his daring foot alight
On the height?
Shall he dwell amidst the humble and the low?

Through what tears and sweat and pain,
Must he gain
Fruitage from the tree of life?
Shall it yield him bitter flavor?
Shall its savor
Be as manna midst the turmoil and the strife?

Through the ages, all mothers have had the same hopes and
fears: the mother of a child born in a manger, the mother of
a son destined to be an emperor.

In his cradle slept and smiled
Thus the child
Who as Prince of Peace was hailed.
Thus anigh the mother breast,
Lulled to rest,
Child-Napoleon down the lilied river sailed.

Crowned or crucified—the same
Glows the flame
Of her deathless love divine.
Still the blessed mother stands,
In all lands,
As she watched beside thy cradle and by mine.

Whatso gifts the years bestow,
Still men know,
While she breathes, lives one who sees
(Stand they pure or sin-defiled)
But the child
Whom she crooned to sleep and rocked upon her knees.

The universality of experience, the kinship of women everywhere: Emma was able to give enduring expression to these feelings. Her sonnet, "Sympathy," like the poem "Loving Mother," has a living, breathing power to appeal to our own age.

> Therefore I dare reveal my private woe,
> The secret blots of my imperfect heart,
> Nor strive to shrink or swell mine own desert,
> Nor beautify nor hide. For this I know,
> That even as I am, thou also art.

In the ordinary tasks of their lives, there is a communion, a sisterhood of common suffering and common joys and achievements that springs up among women everywhere. There is a similarity, a dailiness that is shared—from dustmop despair to family joy, from striving to better their condition to glorying in the essence of womanhood. So one does not seek for sympathy and understanding from those on high, from lives removed from struggle and conflict, but here—next door, to a neighbor, or to one far away, a hand reaches out, and a handclasp is returned in confidence. The poem states it in a few brief lines:

> Thou past heroic forms unmoved shall go,
> To pause and bide with me, to whisper low:
> "Not I alone am weak, not I apart
> Must suffer, struggle, conquer day by day.
> Here is my bosom-sin wherefrom I pray
> Hourly deliverance—this my rose, my thorn.
> This woman my soul's need can understand,
> Stretching o'er silent gulfs her sister hand."

The final line, "stretching o'er silent gulfs her sister hand," echoes across the years. Emma could not consciously have forecast her own future work. But artists constantly sharpen their images, personalize and at the same time generalize them. The image of a woman's hand stretched out in sympathy, in welcome, across far-reaching waters, was to emerge later in Emma's most famous poem written to celebrate the Statue of Liberty.

4

NEW FRIENDS, NEW HORIZONS

❧ It was a brilliant August day, the air shimmering with heat. From her train seat next to the window, Emma could watch the New England countryside unreel before her. The landscape glittered with goldenrod, asters, late roses; farms laid out neat as a patchwork quilt; white church-spires, red barns, the emerald of village greens.

She took out the letter from her bag again—though she already knew every word of it by heart!

After the chagrin of her omission from *Parnassus,* after a year and a half of complete silence, Emerson had written to invite her to "spend a week in Concord and correct our village narrowness."

What an idea—to correct *their* narrowness. She was the one whose horizons were to be expanded!

The great man himself met her at the station, driving up in his one-horse wagon. Though his manner was unassuming, his mere presence denied all notion of ordinariness. Now seventy-three, white-haired and erect, Emerson resembled a patriarch from the Old Testament. Bowing to Emma in his courtly fashion, he introduced her to his wife and daughter Ellen.

Mrs. Emerson was maternally affectionate. Ellen, at thirty-seven, was nearly ten years older than Emma, and a little diffident about their elegantly dressed visitor from New York. She had expected this Miss Lazarus who wrote poetry to look different. What had she expected? She couldn't really say, but somehow she had pictured her as small, a little girl play-acting at being grown up. Now here she was, as Ellen later confided to a friend, "surprisingly mature in appearance and unexpectedly large." Yet she did look a poet, this slender, rather tall woman with dark braids bound about her head with silken ribbons. A few tendrils of hair curled over her forehead, down along her cheeks. Her mouth was full and sensuous, her nose strongly arched, and her eyes—black, intensely glowing. She was full of questions, full of enthusiasm; full of driving life.

Emma's eager questions about Concord, about their neighbors, about the way they lived, were not prying, but genuine interest. She was like an eagle soaring in the world of ideas, Ellen concluded; yes, with her determined, dark brows, the strong cast of her head, she could lift herself into the air by sheer will alone! Wings were necessary only for the more earthbound . . .

Ellen grew fond of Emma as the days went by, finding her "a pleasant—if somewhat intense!—companion."

For Emma it was the most stimulating week of her life. She met Bronson Alcott, the critic; visited with Franklin Benjamin Sanborn and his wife. It was a great occasion for her to meet and talk with Sanborn, who was not only a disciple of Emerson, but an ardent Abolitionist who had acted as New England agent for John Brown. She also met an attractive young man, Thomas Ward, son of the banker at whose house she had first been introduced to Emerson. Tom Ward had accompanied Agassiz on expeditions to Brazil; for Emma, the anecdotes of his travels opened up vistas of an ever-expanding, ever-exciting world.

And there was work to make leisure hours doubly enjoyable. While at the Emersons, she received the proof-sheets of her five-act tragedy in verse, *The Spagnoletto,* set in the Italy of 1655. Emma conceived of it as a play to be read, not to be performed.

It was a week so crowded with events and impressions that Emma kept a journal, a permanent record of "persons that pass and shadows that remain."

There was the Emerson house: "gray, square, with dark green blinds, set amidst noble trees." Her hostess was "stately, white-haired." And there was "the beautiful, faithful Ellen, whose figure seems always to stand by the side of her august father . . ." Concord itself was "lovely and smiling, with its quiet meadows, quiet slopes, and quietest of rivers."

She described an afternoon spent with the poet and biographer of Thoreau, William Ellery Channing. "Generally crabbed and reticent with strangers, he took a liking to me. The bond of our sympathy was my admiration for Thoreau, whose memory he actually worships, having been his companion in his best days, and his daily attendant in the last years of illness and heroic suffering. I do not know whether I was most touched by the thought of the unique, lofty character that had inspired this depth and fervor of friendship, or by the pathetic constancy and pure affection of the poor, desolate old man before me, who tried to conceal his tenderness and sense of irremediable loss by a show of gruffness and philosophy."

The scene was vivid. "I sat with him in the sunlit wood, looking at the gorgeous blue and silver summer sky. He guided me through the woods and pointed out the site of Thoreau's famous hut. A few steps beyond is the pond with thickly-wooded shores—everything exquisitely peaceful and beautiful in the afternoon light, and not a sound to be heard except the crickets or the 'z-ing' of the locusts which Thoreau has described. Farther on he pointed out to me, in the distant land-scape, a low roof, the only one visible, which was the roof of Thoreau's birthplace. He had been over there many times, he said, since he lost Mr. Thoreau. (He never speaks of Thoreau's death, but always 'Thoreau's loss' or 'when I lost Mr. Thoreau'. . . .) But he had never gone in—he was afraid it might look lonely! Instead, he often sat on a rock in front of the house and looked at it."

When Emma left Concord, Channing gave her a package as a parting gift: his own book on Thoreau, and Thoreau's pocket compass used on his walking excursions. It was an affecting gift; Emma choked back tears of gratitude as she shook hands farewell with the devoted scholar. The compass was a talisman, a keepsake of the wonderful week spent under the Emersons' hospitable roof.

Obviously, Emma had the sympathy and understanding that inspires friendship. Yet there was a strand of shyness woven like a pearl-gray thread through her relationships. We can see it in the letter she wrote to Ellen Emerson not long after her return from Concord. "Thank you very much for your kind, welcome letter—I am so glad you sent it just as you did, with the interrupted fragments on different dates, for it was especially pleasant to be reassured of your frequent thoughts of me. I think I require more expressions of friendship from those I care for than most people do—not from any lack of confidence in their kindness or loyalty, but from my painful mistrust of my own capacity to inspire friendship."

Interestingly, and typical of Emma Lazarus' love of life, the letter then goes on in a gay mood, to chat of their many mutual friends, of the current scene, of literature.

The following summer Emma spent in fashionable Newport with her father and sisters. Returning to New York in the fall of 1887, Moses Lazarus moved with his children to a new house, farther uptown, at 34 East Fifty-seventh Street. Emma recalled the years in the house on Fourteenth Street when her mother was alive. Packing up china, silverware, books, ornaments—every article was a memory urgent and insistent. She wrote to Ellen: "It is with the deepest regret that we find ourselves forced to break up the house we have been occupying for the past twenty years, but there is no help for it."

Never one to brood over misfortune, she resumed immediately: "Are you ever coming to New York? How dearly I should love to see your kind friendly face once more! I have seen Tom Ward and he speaks as usual affectionately of you."

Settling into the new house, Emma went back to her writ-

ing, to reading, to social calls, to theatre, lectures, art galleries,
concerts. The winter passed swiftly; she could scarcely believe
that 1878 was already arriving. On New Year's Day, the Lazaruses held open house. Friends,
acquaintances, many of them with eminent names, dropped in.
Emma was becoming familiar with outstanding personalities of
the times. She talked well and her letters have the sparkling
quality of her conversation. She came to be considered "the
best female conversationalist of her day . . . always on fire
about something!"

There was leaping wit along with the fire; sometimes reflected in her poetry. It showed itself in the neatly turned sonnet "Critic And Poet," perhaps directed at Bronson Alcott, for
whose opinions she did not share Emerson's high regard; but
there were plenty of other heavy, solemn-footed judges around
—Emma used an anonymous quotation as her theme.

She simply put the remark in parentheses at the top of her own
lines. ("*Poetry must be simple, sensuous or impassioned; this
man is neither simple, sensuous nor impassioned; therefore he is
not a poet.*")

Her sonnet poked fun at such pretentious logic.

> *No man had ever heard a nightingale,*
> *When once a keen-eyed naturalist was stirred*
> *To study and define—what is a bird,*
> *To classify by rote and book, nor fail*
> *To mark its structure and to note the scale*
> *Whereon its song might possibly be heard.*
> *Thus far, no farther;—so he spake the word.*
> *When of a sudden,—hark, the nightingale!*
>
> *Oh deeper, higher than he could divine*
> *That all-unearthly, untaught strain! He saw*
> *The plain, brown warbler, unabashed. "Not mine"*
> *(He cried) "the error of this fatal flaw.*
> *No bird is this, it soars beyond my line,*
> *Were it a bird, 'twould answer to my law.*

In her image of the nightingale and the studious bird-watcher, Emma expressed her feeling that art has the power to transcend all the laws and rules made up for it. Sometimes the plodding critic cannot understand a new talent that flies upon the horizon; because he cannot understand it, he denies its existence—but the talent goes right on flying.

Emma's lines may have struck home uncomfortably in not a few highly-placed editorial chairs. Being human, she must have been pleased that she had deflated several cushions of complacency.

The moods of her poetry varied. She was inspired by Beethoven's last days, by his heroic struggle against the death of his creative genius.

She submitted her verses to the *Independent*, Henry Ward Beecher's non-denominational weekly. She was amazed at the prominent position the paper awarded her, the entire front page!

As her interests spread in range she began to alternate the writing of verse with critical essays, book reviews, the short story form, articles on prominent artistic personalities. For her all the arts were related.

Still, she was not satisfied with her achievement. She was too honest a person not to see how far she had yet to travel on the road to enduring literature.

She corresponded with other writers, hoping to find clues in their methods of work.

John Burroughs, the naturalist, wrote eagerly: "If I had known all this time would elapse without my seeing you again, I should not have denied myself the pleasure of answering your very agreeable letter long ago. I liked you so much that I have wanted to see more of you and have more talk. I think we have much in common and would get on famously together. You may have heard that we had a plan to have Mr. Whitman come to New York to lecture about the middle of this month. I saw him and spent a day and a night with him four weeks ago. I spoke of you to him. He remembered your name and had read and remarked some of your poems. They had arrested his attention, which you may consider a compliment. . . . I hope also that you are not judging yourself so harshly. I think you need above all things to cherish and insist upon yourself."

A short time later, Burroughs wrote again: "We shall soon get to be correspondents at this rate! I find it very easy and pleasant to write to you, and hope to prove to myself again before long that it is still more easy and pleasant to talk to you. . . . I am delighted to hear that you are equal to the task of appreciating Democratic Vistas. I have not before found a woman that was, and but few men. . . ."

So Emma was a rare, free spirit who did not draw back prudishly from Whitman's all-embracing emotions. She accepted Burroughs' left-handed compliment for the approval it sincerely meant to convey. But she could not help sighing.

She did not want to be an exceptional woman, a person apart. She wanted to belong to womankind, to all humanity. No writer, she maintained, can be truly important who keeps his distance from the world. So she argued with her friend the noted editor, Edmund Clarence Stedman, who lived nearby. They had frequent discussions and clashes of opinion.

One day Emma was in a gloomy mood. Seeing a poem of hers in print, in *Lippincott's,* it seemed trivial to her, of no permanent value. "I have accomplished nothing to stir, nothing to awaken, to teach or to suggest, nothing that the world could not equally well do without."

Stedman smiled at her youthful seriousness. But Emma was not in a light frame of mind. She meant what she said.

Her friend was startled at such brave objectivity. Very well, if she wanted to discuss the matter on that realistic basis, he would admit that he agreed with her own severe judgment. And, she would never become a more meaningful writer if she continued to follow a pattern that was little more than art for art's sake. Classical themes, landscapes, occasional pieces suggested by her reading: these were nothing more than whim. Sometimes the reader's feelings happened to be attuned; but generally the audience was narrowed down to a few special souls.

Fortunately, Emma's reactions were healthy. The feelings she expressed in her poetry could be shared by many. But these feelings were not deep, or universal—in her own words, the world could do without them.

But it was nothing to be gloomy about, Stedman told her. There were many competent writers content with art for art's sake. There was room for all kinds of talent. If Emma continued along her same path, she would continue to be published, to be well-received.

That was not what Emma wanted. It had to be art for the sake of life.

But what life? What could she hope to reflect of reality? Physically, hers was a life of ease. She did not have to toil in a factory. Her strength and youth were not drained in domestic drudgery. She was not cooking, cleaning, baking, sewing, washing, nursing, rearing ten or twelve children (as was not at all uncommon at the time).

Of what kind of life could she write?

Stedman looked at her keenly. "Have you never thought of your own heritage?" he asked quietly.

Emma was puzzled.

"I mean your Jewish heritage. There is a wealth of tradition you are heir to, and could use as a source of inspiration."

Emma had written a few youthful poems with a Jewish background, but she did not think of herself as a Jewish writer. She was an American! "No," she declared, "I am proud of my blood and lineage, but Hebrew ideals do not appeal to me."

Stedman was silent. Perhaps Emma could be convinced with further argument. But every writer, every person, bears responsibility for his own way of life. No one else can choose it for him.

5

DAUGHTER OF HER PEOPLE

🌷 At the time of Emma Lazarus' birth, the number of Jews in the entire United States was some fifty thousand out of a population of twenty-three million—a ratio of approximately one Jew to four hundred non-Jews. By the end of the 1870's, the proportion had grown: three hundred thousand out of a general population of about fifty million, (one Jew to about 170 non-Jews). They had had a corresponding rise in middle-class comfort.

So it was not out of a sense of scorn, but out of a sense of her own lack of emotional feeling that she replied in 1877 to a request by Dr. Gustav Gottheil, Rabbi of Temple Emanu-El of New York, to translate some Jewish hymns from the German for a new hymnal he was compiling. And would she also compose some original ones herself?

"I have translated three of the hymns, and enclose them to you. Is it worthwhile for me to go on, and try the others in this way? As for writing hymns myself, 'the flesh is willing, but the spirit is weak.' I should be most happy to serve you in your difficult and patriotic undertaking, but the more I see of these religious poems, the more I feel that the fervor and enthusiasm requisite to their production are altogether lacking in me."

A few weeks later, she added further protestation. "You need not reproach yourself with having 'forced' upon me an uncongenial work. I cheerfully offered to help you to the extent of my ability, and was glad to prove to you that my interest and sympathies were loyal to our race, although my religious connections (if such they can be called) and the circumstances of my life have led me somewhat apart from our people. I shall still be pleased to try a few more translations, if you will send or bring me the original poems and if I may do them at my leisure."

Incidentally, her brief P. S. is touching. "Please address your notes to me as 'Miss Emma Lazarus.' I have not the honor of being 'Miss Lazarus.'" Only the eldest daughter was entitled to that salutation.

Emma was, as we have seen from her earliest work, aware of her Jewish heritage. The number of verses on Jewish themes began to mount.

And there was her growing interest—a purely literary one, she might have insisted—in the writings of the Hebrew poets of medieval Spain. She was sharply aware of the timeliness— as well as the timelessness—of Solomon Ben Judah Gabirol's poetic message written in the eleventh century. Working from the German version of Michael Sachs and Abraham Geiger, Emma translated his lines, found his original centuries-old title as apt in contemporary English:

A DEGENERATE AGE

Where is the man who has been tried and found strong and sound?
Where is the friend of reason and knowledge?
I see only skeptics and weaklings.
I see only prisoners in the durance of the senses.
And every fool and every spendthrift
Thinks himself as great a master as Aristotle.
Think'st thou that they have written poems?
Call'st thou that a song?
I call it the cackling of ravens,
The zeal of the prophet must free poesy
From the embrace of wanton youths.
My song I have inscribed on the forehead of Time,
They know and hate it—for it is lofty.

She, too, would like to inscribe her song on the forehead of Time. Communing with her own conscience, she translated Gabirol's "Night-Thoughts":

> . . . What is the pleasure of the day for me,
> If, in its crucible, I must renew
> Incessantly the pangs of purifying?
> Up, challenge, wrestle, and o'ercome! Be strong!
> The late grapes cover all the vines with fruit.
> I am not glad, though even the lion's pride
> Content itself upon the field's poor grass.
> My spirit sinks beneath the tide, soars not
> With fluttering sea mews on the moist, soft strand.
> I follow Fortune not, where'er she lead.
> Lord o'er myself, I banish her, compel,
> And though her clouds should rain no blessed dew,
> Though she withold the crown, the heart's desire,
> Though all deceive, though honey change to gall,
> Still am I lord, and will in freedom strive.

(Later, in 1881, these translations from the Spanish Hebrew poets were published by the *Jewish Messenger*.)

"Though honey change to gall . . . still am I lord o'er myself and will in freedom strive." Like the obstinately surviving spirit of the Jews, Emma began to take a strengthened pride in her heritage. Encouraged by Rabbi Gottheil, and impelled by the writings of the medieval Hebrew poets, she started to study history more earnestly, to learn from it lessons for today.

After reading about the decree of the Lateran Council of 1215, she wrote "Guardian Of The Red Disk: Spoken by a Citizen of Malta, 1300." In stinging lines, she described how the Jews of Malta were forced to wear a red, wheel-shaped badge signifying infamy; and how Christian guardians were appointed to make sure the decree was carried out; how "the scarlet stamp of separateness, of shame" was printed on the chin of every Jew. The pious, who wore beards, had to bear the imprint on the cheek.

She next wrote a long, ambitious work based on Jewish history: *The Dance To Death*, a verse-drama in five acts, laid in the Germany of the Middle Ages. The year is 1349, the scene the Free City of Nordhausen where the Jews are living unmolested, at peace with their neighbors.

But a fearful pestilence has been spreading across Europe. The Jews are accused of poisoning the wells and of causing the Black Plague. They are condemned to be burned: "All, Jews, Jewesses and Jewlings."

One of the central characters is a young woman forced to choose between her personal love and loyalty to her doomed people. She cries out: "O God! How shall I pray for strength to love him less than mine own soul! No more of that. I am all Israel's now. Till this cloud pass, I have no thought, no passion, no desire, save for my people."

Susskind, a wealthy Jewish merchant, has pleaded for his people—but in vain. He addresses the Council of the city:

> . . . Have mercy on us, we are innocent,
> Who are brothers, husbands, fathers, sons as ye!
> Look you, we have dwelt among you many years,
> Led thrifty, peaceable, well-ordered lives.
> Who can attest, who prove we ever wrought
> Or ever did devise the smallest harm,
> Far less this fiendish crime against the State!
> Rather let those arise who owe the Jews
> Some debt of unpaid kindness, profuse alms,
> The Hebrew leech's serviceable skill,
> Who know our patience under injury,
> And ye would see, if all stood bravely forth,
> A motley host . . .
>
> . . . .
>
> We know the Black Death is a scourge of God.
> Is not our flesh as capable of pain,
> Our blood as quick envenomed as your own?
> Has the Destroying Angel passed the posts
> Of Jewish doors—to visit Christian homes?
> We all are slaves of one tremendous Hour.
> We drink the waters which our enemies say
> We spoil with poison,—we must breathe, as ye,
> The universal air,—we droop, faint, sicken,
> From the same causes to the selfsame end.

But reason is useless. The Council head cuts him off: "No more, no more! Go, bid your tribe make ready for their death at sunset."

To die that very day? Susskind cannot believe such cruelty
possible, even from his enemies. He beseeches once more:

> At set of sun today?
> Why, if you travelled to the nighest town,
> Summoned to stand before a mortal Prince,
> You would need longer grace to put in order
> Household effects, to bid farewell to friends,
> And make yourself right worthy. But our way
> Is long, our journey difficult, our judge
> Of awful majesty. Must we set forth,
> Haste-flushed and unprepared? One brief day more,
> And all my wealth is yours!

The Council is adamant: "We have heard enough. Begone,
and bear our message."

So Susskind leaves, to take back the dreadful finality of the
decree:

> Our fate is sealed. These tigers are athirst.
> Return we to our people to proclaim
> The gracious sentence of the noble court.
> Let us go thank the Lord who made us those
> To suffer, not to do, this deed. Be strong. . . .
> Oh let us die as warriors of the Lord. . . .
> Hark ye! Let us crave one boon
> At our assassins' hands; beseech them build
> Within God's acre where our fathers sleep,
> A dancing-floor to hide the faggots stacked.
> Then let the minstrels strike the harp and lute,
> And we will dance and sing above the pile,
> Fearless of death, until the flames engulf,
> Even as David danced before the Lord,
> As Miriam danced and sang beside the sea. . . .

The strange request is granted. The dancing-floor is built,
the burning pyre is also erected. As the hour of the dance to
death approaches, Susskind proclaims his vision:

> I see, I see
> How Israel's ever-crescent glory makes
> These flames that would eclipse it, dark as blots
> Of candle-light against the blazing sun.
> We die a thousand deaths,—drown, bleed, and burn;

Our ashes are dispersed unto the winds.
Yet the wild winds cherish the sacred seed,
The waters guard it in their crystal heart,
The fire refuseth to consume. It springs,
A tree immortal, shadowing many lands,
Unvisited, unnamed, undreamed as yet.

Even as we die in honor, from our death
Shall bloom a myriad heroic lives,
Brave through our bright example, virtuous
Lest our great memory fall in disrepute.
Is one among us brothers, would exchange
His doom against our tyrants,—lot for lot?
Let him go forth and live—he is no Jew.
Let him go forth—
He may die full of years upon his bed.
Ye who nurse rancor haply in your hearts,
Fear ye we perish unavenged? Not so!
Today, no! nor tomorrow! but in God's time,
Our witnesses arise. Ours is the truth,
Ours is the power, the gift of Heaven. We hold
His Law, His lamp, His covenant, His pledge.
Wherever in the ages shall arise
Jew-priest, Jew-poet, Jew-singer, or Jew-saint—
And everywhere I see them star the gloom—
In each of these the martyrs are avenged!

The moment has come. The Rabbi carries the sacred articles
of the Synagogue to the funeral pyre, "the bell-fringed, silken-
bound Scroll of the Law. Gather the silver vessels, dismantle
the rich curtains of the doors, bring the Perpetual Lamp; all
these shall burn . . ."

And in the final scene, the doors of the Synagogue are burst
open. The crowd howls:

> *Come forth! the sun sets. Come, the Council waits!*
> *What! will ye teach your betters patience? Out!*
> *The Governor is ready. Forth with you,*
> *Curs! serpents! Judases! The bonfire burns!*

Like her earlier play in verse, *The Spagnoletto,* Emma did
not conceive *The Dance to Death* as a drama to be performed.
Although she must have realized that this new work was vastly

superior to the earlier one, she did not submit it anywhere
for publication. Parts of it were so strong, so powerful, they did
not seem to belong with the body of her work. Strange, as
though in wrestling with her conscience, another voice was
calling, another mind operating. She put the drama into a desk
drawer; showed it to no one.

By now her work was becoming widely read; still she remained unsatisfied. She was contributing essays and poetry to the
Century and to the *Critic,* the two leading magazines of the
times. The period of the Eighteen-Seventies was drawing to a
close.

The *Century,* in its farewell issue of the decade, featured
"Poems by American Women," including one by Emma Lazarus, "The Taming of the Falcon." The tamer's influence
appears complete, then is forgotten when the bird flies away.
Was the bird a female fledgling, longing to be free of a male-
dominated society? Was it a new literary world seeking release
from old European values? Was the bird a Jewish spirit looking
for identification among its own kind? And if the bird was
Emma herself flying upward on unbound wings—where was
the freedom towards which she hoped to soar?

As time passed, Stedman's words of advice: to use her own
Jewish heritage for inspiration, echoed insistently in her mind.
But how to use it most effectively? She had gone back to the
dark archives of history, and while lights glimmered there in
the depths, there was not a broad enough pathway there, no
steady radiance to illuminate the present. The beacon-star of
Emerson's influence had long since faded. Where was a spark,
a continuing gleam to be found? The past was heavy and bur-
densome: she sought for identification nearer her own time.

In June of 1881, not signing her name, perhaps because of
her sex, she contributed an important editorial article, "American Literature," to the *Critic,* distinguished fortnighly review
of all the arts. Lashing out at those who denied that any con-

tinuous national tradition was developing in American literature, her editorial traced the line of Emerson, marking "the flowering of a distinctly American school of thought and habit of life—followed by Thoreau and John Burroughs, Hawthorne's *Scarlet Letter,* Walt Whitman, James Russell Lowell, Oliver Wendell Holmes, Bret Harte. . . ."

This was a subject Emma had dealt with earlier in her poem "How Long?" Informally, on the same theme, she wrote to Thomas Wentworth Higginson: "For my part, I absolutely refuse to share the 'low down' estimate of our national literature which the Anglo-American and half-informed Englishman are inclined to make. To my eyes, there are signs of fresh vitality in every direction."

The responsibility of the writer, his sources of inspiration, his links to his people and country—in these ideas she took a keen interest. Her old friend and mentor, Stedman, was editing an anthology to be called *Poetry in America.* He sent the manuscript of his introductory essay to Emma to read and criticize, while it was still in the manuscript stage, so great was his respect for her judgment.

Emma replied promptly. "I have been thinking a great deal over your *Poetry in America,* and having been so frank with you, I feel it on my conscience to tell you the one point on which I cannot quite agree with you. I do not think the absence of a great national poet either in Colonial Revolutionary days, or at the present time, can be adequately accounted for even by the extremely adverse conditions which you state in so clear and masterly a manner. . . ."

Stedman insisted that there was no free-flowing song in the New World, and marshalled arguments to bolster his stand. "The colonial restriction," he maintained, "made the western lyre a mechanism to echo, without fresh and true feeling, notes that came from over the sea. . . . It may be that the people had no real need of poets; and song and art, like invention, come not

without necessity. . . . The art of writing verse was almost solely
a luxury of the professional classes, and . . . it is not to the
wigged and gowned that we instinctively listen for the music
and freedom of creative song. . . . [Our republican system] is
a leveller, and in its early stages, raises a multitude to the level
of the commonplace. . . . The general independence and comfort
have not bred those dramatic elements which imply conditions
of splendor and squalor, glory and shame, triumph and despair
. . . In no other country are there so many happy little house-
holds. . . . [creative energy went instead into] the peerless
exploits of our engineers, capitalists, discoverers. . . ."

"No," Emma answered Stedman, "these may explain the
dearth of poets as a class, but I do not think they would have
any real weight with that altogether phenomenal and divinely
inspired being whom we think of as the great poet—Dante,
Shakespeare, Aeschylus, Milton—etc."

Further, in contrasting America and other countries, Stedman
had written: "Look at Scotland. Her national melodies were
ready and waiting for Burns; her legends, history, traditions, for
Walter Scott."

Emma contested this: "Now that Burns and Scott have
poetized all the Scotch legends, traditions and national Songs,
it is easy to say, 'These were ready at hand, waiting for their
poet.' But how long did they have to wait? Until these clear-
eyed seers were born, whoever thought the rich patois of the
grim old highlander and the barbarous music of the bagpipes
could be associated in our minds with romance and melody?"

Nor could she hold with another of Stedman's contentions,
that while lyric poets could write from their own emotion and
experiences, poets who wanted to use larger forms "often have
been arrested . . . by a scarcity of home-themes, no less than by
the lack of sharp dramatic contrast in equable American life. . . ."

Emma replied: "I never have believed in the want of a theme
—wherever there is humanity, there is the theme for a great
poem—and I think it is the poet's fault if he does not know

how to utilize the accessories and materials which surround him. All you say is wise, keen, and absolutely true of American poetry—but if the Genius had been born, I cannot help believing, all these objections and impediments would have been blown to the winds with the first sweep of his lyre. I shall not apologize for speaking to you so candidly, but when you gave me your Essay to read, I am sure you wanted to hear not what the world has proved to you so often already, that you are yourself an artist and a guide—but rather how your carefully elaborated and important thoughts may strike another mind that views things from a somewhat different angle."

Wherever there is humanity there is a theme. Her own words, and Stedman's advice, echoed over and over. Her particular segment of humanity, her Jewishness—here was surely a valid theme, yet how could she conceive of herself as a "poet of her people"? She did not have that strong an identification, that burning a feeling about her status. True, she had sung of the past, but one lives in the present and must be aroused by life around. Perplexed, she turned to another Jewish poet who was also concerned with his Jewishness, and who also protested that he was concerned only in a literary way. She steeped herself in the life and work of Heinrich Heine, whose brilliant career had been so tragically cut short by death. Earlier, she had translated his ironic ballad, "Donna Clara," into crisp, terse lines:

> In the evening through her garden
> Wanders the Alcalde's daughter;
> Festal sounds of drum and trumpet
> Ring out hither from the castle.

> "I am weary of the dances,
> Honeyed words of adulation
> From the knights who still compare me
> To the sun with dainty phrases.

> "Yes, of all things I am weary,
> Since I first beheld by moonlight,
> Him my cavalier, whose zither
> Nightly draws me to my casement.

"As he stands, so slim and daring,
  With his flaming eyes that sparkle
  From his nobly-pallid features,
  Truly he St. George resembles."

Thus went Donna Clara dreaming,
  On the ground her eyes were fastened,
  When she raised them, lo! before her
  Stood the handsome, knightly stranger.

Pressing hands and whispering passion,
  These twain wander in the moonlight.
  Gently doth the breeze caress them,
  The enchanted roses greet them.

The enchanted roses greet them,
  And they glow like love's own heralds;
  "Tell me, tell me, my belovèd,
  Wherefore, all at once thou blushest."

"Gnats were stinging me, my darling,
  And I hate these gnats in summer,
  E'en as though they were a rabble
  Of vile Jews with long, hooked noses."

"Heed not gnats nor Jews, belovèd,"
  Spake the knight with fond endearments.
  From the almond-tree dropped downward
  Myriad snowy flakes of blossoms.

Myriad snowy flakes of blossoms
  Shed around them fragrant odors.
  "Tell me, tell me, my belovèd,
  Looks thy heart on me with favor?"

"Yes, I love thee, oh my darling,
  And I swear it by our Savior,
  Whom the accursed Jews did murder
  Long ago with wicked malice."

"Heed thou neither Jews nor Savior,"
  Spake the knight with fond endearments;
  Far-off waved as in a vision
  Gleaming lilies bathed in moonlight.

Gleaming lilies bathed in moonlight
Seemed to watch the stars above them.
"Tell me, tell me, my belovèd,
Didst thou not erewhile swear falsely?"

"Naught is false in me, my darling,
E'en as in my bosom floweth
Not a drop of blood that's Moorish,
Neither of foul Jewish current."

"Heed not Moors nor Jews, belovèd,"
Spake the knight with fond endearments.
Then towards a grove of myrtles
Leads he the Alcalde's daughter.

And with love's slight, subtle meshes,
He hath trapped her and entangled;
Brief their words, but long their kisses,
For their hearts are overflowing.

What a melting bridal carol,
Sings the nightingale, the pure one!
How the fire-flies in the grasses
Trip their sparkling, torch-light dances!

In the grove the silence deepens;
Naught is heard save furtive rustling
Of the swaying myrtle branches,
And the breathing of the flowers.

But the sound of drum and trumpet
Burst forth sudden from the castle.
Rudely they awaken Clara,
Pillowed on her lover's bosom.

"Hark, they summon me, my darling.
But before I go, oh tell me,
Tell me what thy precious name is,
Which so closely thou hast hidden."

And the knight, with gentle laughter,
Kissed the fingers of his donna,
Kissed her lips and kissed her forehead,
And at last these words he uttered:

"I, Senora, your belovèd,
Am the son of the respected,
Worthy, erudite Grand Rabbi,
Israel of Saragossa!"

Among the notes Heine left at his death were suggestions for
several more narrative poems in the same style. Emma wrote
"Don Pedrillo," based on Heine's own scheme—in which the
son of Donna Clara and the Jew vents forth his hatred of Jews
to a Rabbi he does not know is his own father. She also composed "Fra Pedro"—again following Heine's notes—telling
of how the boy, grown up to be an Abbot, persecutes the Jews.

Emma decided to compile a book of her translations from
Heine, and to introduce it with a biographical study. She became fascinated by the duality of his upbringing, by the "un-
Jewishness" of his Jewishness. Undoubtedly she read into his
life parallels with her own.

She traced the two-sidedness of his education: the young
Heine in Düsseldorf, studying at a lyceum housed in a Fran-
ciscan convent, and at the same time attending a private Jewish
school. She spoke of his activities in the Society for the Culture
and Improvement of the Jews. "He frankly confessed," she
wrote, "that he—'the born enemy of all positive religions'—
was no enthusiast for the Jewish faith, but he was none the
less eager to proclaim himself an enthusiast for the rights of
Jews and their civic equality." And on his consent to baptism,
she commented that it was "only after he had exhausted every
means of endeavoring to secure a remission of the humiliating
decree." (In order to hold office in Prussia, one had to be bap-
tized.)

Poems and Ballads of Heinrich Heine was handsomely received
by the press. Stedman told Emma he had stayed up past mid-
night reading her translations. "They are very subtle and very
spirited."

After having been isolated for so many months with her work on Heine, it was good to vacation for a while at Lenox, the fashionable and popular resort in Massachusetts. After resting there, she traveled about, and returned to Manhattan in late July.

6

THE TORCH UPLIFTED

🌼 In 1879, in Russia, a devastating series of pogroms was launched against the Jewish population. The ancient falsehood—that the Jews were to blame for all woes— was raised with a terrifying tumult; the cries of the beaten and trampled-upon dying away to whispers under the shouts of the persecutors. The pogroms raged on.

Humanity the world over could not condone such cruelty. Protest meetings were called in London. New York could do no less.

Headed by former President Ulysses Grant, a committee was formed in Manhattan, representing all faiths, to "express sympathy with the persecuted Hebrews in the Russian Empire." A mass meeting was arranged for Chickering Hall.

It was a chilly winter night; a sense of wrathful justice took people out of their warm homes and into the cold night. The hall was quickly packed.

Former Secretary of State William Evarts spoke. Emma had met him several times at social gatherings; it was at his personal request that she was attending tonight's meeting.

Evarts mentioned the brutality of the most recent pogroms that had taken place on Christmas Day. ". . . on the morning when, in the name of Christ, peace and good will were proclaimed over all the earth. Without forgetting the glass house in which we ourselves live—we who have seen anti-Negro riots in New York and anti-Chinese riots at San Francisco—it must still be said that Russia's duty is to civilize herself. It is not that it is the oppression of Jews by Russia: it is that it is the oppres-

sion of men and women by men and women; and we are men
and women."

The oppression of men and women by men and women.
Emma went home that night, fired with a sense of urgency.
Her heart suffered for the millions who were being persecuted.
The Jews of Russia were being forced to flee; across the borders
to Germany, across the boundary of Europe to the free world of
America.

With a committee of women, Emma went to Ward's Island
in the East River, where the refugees were being temporarily
housed. There were so many that housing and work could not
be found for all.

They wandered—bearded ancients wearing round black hats
and long black gowns worn rusty green with time; young
rabbinical students with paisses; the unreligious; mothers nursing infants; ragged children; women dressed in men's jackets
that had been given them; men wrapped around with shawls;
merchants and peasants; the robust and the consumptive—tossed
like refuse across the vast ocean.

All these unfortunates must be helped. But not out of pity,
not out of the smug, snug comfort of charity. They must be
helped so that they could walk in the world as human beings
again, erect on their own two feet. Let no time be wasted in
thanking their benefactors; let them arise and stand on their
own merits. She contributed money, helped raise funds from
among her acquaintances for resettling the refugees. For those
who could work, work must be found; and the young must be
sent to school.

Emma communicated with Rabbi Gottheil: "Please find enclosed one hundred dollars from myself and my friend, for the
benefit of our protégé." (This was a young, brilliant scholar
who was being sent to an American university.) "As I understand our agreement, you will add to this sum fifty dollars more,
and deposit the whole amount in safe keeping to be drawn by

him in weekly installments of $10. I wish you would please impress it very emphatically upon his mind that I do not wish it to be known *to anyone but himself* how I have befriended him. I think it best to tell him first what share I have taken in the matter, and to add that this is the only return I ask for such interest as I have manifested in his fate. I rely upon his mentioning *to no one under any circumstances* by whose hands and in what way the effort has been made to assist him out of his present difficulties. . . .

"I thank you most earnestly for my own part, for showing me the way and inspiring me with the courage to carry out my own impulse—which without your assistance and cooperation I should never have been able to accomplish."

How different from her earlier correspondence with the Rabbi —when she felt she could not identify sufficiently with the Jewish cause to contribute to his hymnbook!

In April of 1882, the *Century* magazine carried an article on Disraeli that Emma had written some time before. "Was the Earl of Beaconsfield a Representative Jew?"

Gazing at the title now, she must have felt as though a stranger had written the piece, not herself.

She had almost forgotten it, so caught up had she now become in the problems of the Jewish refugees. Reading over her own words, she felt a troubling dissatisfaction. In how short a time —in the span of just a few months—how greatly her ideas had changed!

". . . Disraeli possessed in an eminent degree the capacity which seems to us the most characteristic feature of the Jew, whether considered as a race or an individual, and one which has been developed to perfection by ages of persecution. We refer to the faculty which enables this people, not only to perceive and make the most of every advantage of their situation and temperament, but also, with marvelous adroitness, to transform their very disabilities into new instruments of power.

Today, in Europe, their commercial prosperity is such as to arouse the jealousy and enmity of nations supposed to be the most enlightened, and yet this excessive accumulation of wealth is only the natural result of the stupid, not to say cruel, policy of those very nations in confining them for years to the practice of usury. Ostracised from the society of Christians, refused a voice in the administration of public affairs, denied the honor of military service, excommunicated at the same time from legal protection and from Christian charity, it behooved them to organize all the more stringently their own little communities, to perfect their system of private beneficence, to administer their own affairs with scrupulous exactness, to practice the arts of peace, and to keep their eyes and wits ever open to the chance of gaining an inch of ground from the common enemy. . . .

"Adroitness, dexterity, tact, industry, perseverance, ambition, brilliancy, and imagination—these may be enumerated as their distinguishing qualities. . . . But in proportion as we seek among the less brilliant avenues to renown, among the slowly rewarded workers and students, we shall find fewer and fewer representatives of the race. . . . Thus far their religion, whose mere preservation under such adverse conditions seems little short of a miracle, has been deprived of the natural means of development and progress, and has remained a stationary force. The next hundred years will, in our opinion, be the test of their vitality as a people; the phase of toleration upon which they are only now entering will prove whether or not they are capable of growth."

Emma flushed. To have written such a glib, superficial piece was bad enough. To have it appear at this time, made it worse.

When history enters, it does so stormily. The same issue of the magazine carried an article by another woman writer: Madame Zinaida Alexievna Ragozin, historian and member of learned societies in Europe. Her article was entitled "Russian Jews and Gentiles: From a Russian Point of View."

Emma read it, could scarcely contain her rage. It was an apologia for the pogroms! The pogroms, according to Madame Ragozin, must be seen in the light of "historical perspective." Where there is smoke, there must be fire. There must be a reason why throughout the ages, people turned against the Jews. Now she, Madame Ragozin, had discovered the real reason. It was that the Jews were "worshippers of the Golden Calf." They robbed the Gentiles, and when the Gentiles fought back, the Jews retreated—for they were more concerned with saving their money than their manly honor. Madame then brought forth her trump card: her authority a Talmudic scholar, a Jew himself, Jacob Brafmann. He had analyzed how words of the sacred Talmud instructed Jews in avarice and cowardice.

Emma was furious. She went directly to Richard Watson Gilder, editor of the *Century*. The very next issue of the magazine must carry a reply to this infamous attack upon the Jews. Who would write it? If need be, she would!

Returning home, she choked down her rage. She needed to think clearly and with calm. She would have to have solid facts. What authority could she consult?

She turned for advice to the noted Hebrew scholar, Michael Heilprin. His scholarship was of almost universal range; he knew twelve languages; and was currently at work on the *New American Cyclopedia*. He also had first-hand experience of persecution. At the age of nineteen, he had fled from Poland to Hungary, where he was active under Kossuth in the Revolution of 1848. Now settled in New York, Heilprin was able to help Emma demolish Madame Ragozin's arguments and her "authority." Jacob Brafmann was a notorious apostate, whose book *The Cabbala* was a vile caricature of the teachings of the Talmud. Heilprin was familiar with Brafmann's distortions, and went over them, point by point, with Emma.

As soon as Emma finished her article, she took it to Gilder, who featured her reply to Madame Ragozin's attack in the next issue of the *Century*.

"Russian Christianity Versus Modern Judaism" was a tempered enough title; Emma's words rang clear and strong with the power of the truth and her emotions. Her article carried an extra burden of conviction, for as it appeared, the proscriptive May Laws were passed in Russia. The pogrom was now stamped with the seal of officialdom, with lawless law. Conditions became even more intolerable for the Jewish population and a new flood of refugees poured into New York harbor.

Readers of the May, 1882, issue of the Century scanned Emma's article thoughtfully. ". . . Let us first disabuse our readers of the sophistical distinction made by Madame Ragozin, in common with many other writers, between the 'two kinds of Jews,' and the idea that 'a vast dualism essentially characterizes this extraordinary race.' Behind this subtle error lurk all the dangers that have threatened the existence of the people, for whatever calumnies be refuted by a Jewish spokesman, the answer is ever ready: 'These charges do not apply to you, and such as you. But how can you be sure that such outrages are not committed by some barbarous sect of your tribe?' Now, we can be sure of the Jews—more so, perhaps, than of any other people in the world, their history being the oldest among civilized nations, their social and moral code having remained unaltered through all time, and the vicissitudes of their fate having exposed them to almost every test which can affect individual or national character. The dualism of the Jews is the dualism of humanity; they are made up of the good and the bad. May not Christendom be divided into those Christians who denounce such outrages as we are considering, and those who commit or apologize for them? Immortal genius and moral purity, as exemplified by Moses and Spinoza, constitute a minority among the Jews, as they do among the Gentiles, but here ends the truth of the matter. . . .

"There is but one answer to the charges against the Jews, which Brafmann professes to base upon quotations from the Talmud: they are singly and collectively false. They have not even the doubtful merit of originality, being simply a revamping of the wearisome old perversions, garblings, distortions, mistranslations of the spirit and letter of the text, which have been fully refuted by documents familiar to the whole reading public. For the subtle meaning of the Talmud we need not go to a bribed renegade and thief, who had the documents 'abstracted' for him 'not without danger, by a friend from the Jewish archives.' Charges of a similar nature to Mr. Brafmann's, but incomparably worse, were satisfactorily refuted two hundred years ago by Manassah ben-Israel, in his famous petition to Oliver Cromwell.

"If a Moslem were to print an expurgated copy of the Bible, citing all the barbarous passages and omitting all the humane and noble features, what would Islam think of the cornerstone of Christianity? Yet this is precisely what the Jew-haters have done with the Talmud. Modern philosophical criticism, no less than a study of Jewish history, and a dawning appreciation of the nobility of the Jewish type of character, have dispelled among all thinking and cultivated minds the web of calumny spun by bigotry and folly around these remarkable volumes. . . .

"Madame Ragozin says the Jews are hated not because of different race, religion, dress, peculiar customs, etc., but because of their 'servility, their abjectness, their want of manliness, their failure to stand up for themselves and resent injuries.' Any one who aims at being as strictly logical as Madame Ragozin might know that it is in vain to expect the virtues of freemen from a community of slaves. Of this same people, a prominent American Christian clergyman (Rev. Dr. Howard Crosby) publicly declared a few weeks ago: 'It is the glory of America that she finds among the Israelites the purest and strongest elements of republican liberty.'

". . . is it not as puerile as it is monstrous to assert that the Christians, who outnumber the Jews by millions, who have the whole power of the law and the throne to back them, not to speak of the prejudice of the whole civilized world in their favor, can find no other weapons than tyranny, violence, and murder to preserve them against the Jew, who has nothing but his wits? . . .

" 'Down with the Jews!' say the Loyalists; 'they are at the bottom of Nihilism!' 'Down with the Jews and all the property-holding classes!' yell the Nihilists. 'When the pitcher falls upon the stone,' says the Talmud, 'woe unto the pitcher! When the stone falls upon the pitcher, woe unto the pitcher! Whatever befalls, woe unto the pitcher!' . . ."

Emma had been looking for a light to guide her. She had it clear before her now: the cause of the oppressed. Her light would never be extinguished.

7

BURNING BRIGHT

🌸 Now Emma's hours for work could not be long enough, her pen could not race swiftly enough across the pages. Lines she composed flashed like sword-blades in sunlight for the Jewish cause. Emma would help raise standards out of the Jews' own fiercely proud heritage. And out of her own heritage, too: she shared in it as well. A surge of intense pride, of belonging, coursed through her as she realized now the truth of Stedman's words.

Using the thrilling story of the Maccabean revolt, she wrote "The Banner of the Jew." Scenes paled by history sprang newly alive as Emma recalled Mattathias, and his five sons— Jonathan, known as the Wise; John, whose name meant the Elect; Eleazer, the Help-of-God; Simon, the Burst-of-Spring or Jewel; and Judas, the Prince. For eleven long years, from 175- 164 B.C., they led the people of Palestine against the tyrannical power of Antiochus IV ruling a portion of the Greek empire Alexander had established in Asia. And out of that struggle came victory.

THE BANNER OF THE JEW

Wake, Israel, wake! Recall today
The glorious Maccabean rage,
The sire heroic, hoary-gray,
His five-fold lion-lineage:
The Wise, the Elect, the Help-of-God,
The Burst-of-Spring, the Avenging Rod.

From Mizpeh's mountain-ridge they saw
Jerusalem's empty streets, her shrine
Laid waste where Greeks profaned the law,

68

With idol and with pagan sign.
Mourners in tattered black were there,
With ashes sprinkled on their hair.

Then from the stony peak there rang
A blast to ope the graves: down poured
The Maccabean clan, who sang
Their battle-anthem to the Lord.
Five heroes lead, and following, see,
Ten thousand rush to victory!

Oh for Jerusalem's trumpet now,
To blow a blast of shattering power,
To wake the sleepers high and low,
And rouse them to the urgent hour!
No hand for vengeance—but to save,
A million naked swords should wave.

O deem not dead that martial fire,
Say not the mystic flame is spent!
With Moses' law and David's lyre,
Your ancient strength remains unbent.
Let but an Ezra rise anew,
To lift the Banner of the Jew!

A rag, a mock at first—erelong,
When men have bled and women wept,
To guard its precious folds from wrong,
Even they who shrunk, even they who slept,
Shall leap to bless it, and to save.
Strike! for the brave revere the brave!

The poem was read aloud at the closing exercise of the Temple Emanu-El Religious School in New York; then printed in the pages of the *Critic;* reprinted the following week in the *American Hebrew.* "The Banner Of The Jew" was quoted in living rooms, halls, pulpits. John Greenleaf Whittier declared "it had the ring of Israel's war trumpets."

What a short step measured by time—what an enormous stride measured by the mind's journey. As she was fired by a cause, by conscience, so Emma's poetry now rose to heights.

Romantic images, superfluous adjectives were gone. Her lines
needed no cheapening adornments. Content and form fused into
a unifying whole.

Once themes from the history of the Jews were little closer to
her than themes from Greek and Roman mythology or medieval
legend. Now, every literary theme became permeated with a
consciousness of her people. Longfellow had died in March;
Emma wrote an article evaluating his contribution to American
literature. A memorial meeting honoring the nationally esteemed
poet was held at the Young Men's Hebrew Association where,
early in April, Emma's paper was read aloud.

She viewed Longfellow as belonging "intellectually and
artistically to the generation of Washington Irving, rather than
to that of his actual contemporaries, Emerson or Walt Whitman;
all his links are with the past; the legendary, the historic, enchanted him with an irresistible glamor; not only was he without
the eyes of the seer, to penetrate the well of the future, but
equally without the active energy or the passionate enthusiasm of
an inspired champion in the arena of the present. . . ."

Was she reproaching her own past, along with Longfellow?
She acknowledged the genuine contribution he had made: he
had "a pensive gentleness, a fluent grace, a tender sympathy with
the weak, the suffering, the oppressed, with loving women and
with little children, and above all, an exquisite delicacy of taste,
and an admirable skill of workmanship—these are the distinguishing characteristics of his poetry. . . ."

But she could not resist reference to a poem that had special
meaning for her, since she, too, had written on the same subject.
The Longfellow verses troubled her.

"It is scarcely necessary," she wrote, "to recall to Jewish
hearers the well known lines, 'In the Jewish Cemetery at Newport,' wherein Longfellow's tender humanity finds sweet and
pathetic expression. These lines, in their almost colloquial simplicity, and their use of sacred, legendary or symbolic terms

for purposes of homely illustration, are very characteristic of his method. . . . Jewish readers will not be so willing to accept the concluding stanzas of the poem:

> *And thus forever with reverted look*
> *The mystic volume of the world they read,*
> *Spelling it backward like a Hebrew book,*
> *Till life became a legend of the Dead.*
>
> *But ah! what once has been shall be no more!*
> *The groaning earth in travail and in pain*
> *Brings forth its races, but does not restore,*
> *And the dead nations never rise again.*

"The rapidly increasing influence of the Jews in Europe, the present universal agitation of the Jewish question, hotly discussed in almost every pamphlet, periodical and newspaper of the day, the frightful wave of persecution directed against the race, sweeping over the whole civilized world and reaching its height in Russia, the furious zeal with which they are defended and attacked, the suffering, privation and martyrdom which our brethren still consent to undergo in the name of Judaism, prove them to be very warmly and thoroughly alive, and not at all in need of miraculous resuscitation to establish their nationality. . . ."

Caught up in her new-found cause, the past tugged with nostalgic pain. In April of 1882, Emerson died; she wrote to his daughter, her friend: "My dear Ellen—How much I have thought of you and wondered how your brave and cheerful spirit was enduring the long-dreaded event. Yesterday I saw Tom Ward who told me you were calm and well, and I write today simply to send you my most affectionate greetings and to say how constantly my heart has been with you and your dear Mother. As for that transfigured soul that has passed away, I dare not speak. We can only honor ourselves in praising or commemorating him. I am thankful indeed to know that the

end was so peaceful and serene—and that even with this you
need not associate the thought of bitterness or pain—"

Emma commemorated his spirit in an article for the *Century*,
entitled "Emerson's Personality." "He is the splendid antithesis
of all that is mean and blameworthy in our politics and pursuits," she wrote, "for he also is the legitimate outcome of
American institutions, and affords an eternal refutation of the
fallacy that democracy is fatal to the production and nurture
of the highest chivalry, philosophy, and virtue."

It was late June, 1882. New York was unpleasantly warm,
the air gritty with dust. But Emma had no desire to leave the
city for the refreshing breezes of Long Island or Newport as in
former summers. Destitute and bewildered, thousands of her
fellow-Jews kept arriving in increasing numbers. She could not
abandon them.

She went back again and again to Ward's Island to cheer new
arrivals with gifts of food, clothing, money. From where they
huddled in the temporary shelters like ragged gray bundles, she
returned home to pour her heart out in writing. Her tears became
tears of anger against injustice; she sang no dirge, but a call to
courage.

In her historical reading, she came across an episode from
fifteenth-century Spain. A Jew, converted to Catholicism, had
risen in the Church to the position and power of a bishop. A
former friend—who remained a Jew—wrote a letter to him,
filled with seemingly innocent questions, but each a sharpened
arrow to sting the conscience of the convert. Emma composed
a poem based upon the actual letter. Although it is more than
thirty stanzas long it moves so rapidly and with such scornful
wit that the reader is catapulted along with it.

AN EPISTLE

*From Joshua Ibn Vives of Allorqui to his Former
Master, Solomon Levi-Paul, De Santa-Maria, Bishop of
Cartagena, Chancellor of Castile, and Privy Councillor
to King Henry III of Spain:*

VI

For I, they servant, gather in one sheaf
  The venomed shafts of slander, which thy word
Shall shrivel to small dust. If haply grief,
  Or momentary pain, I deal, my Lord,
Blame not thy servant's zeal, nor be thou deaf
  Unto my soul's blind cry for light. Accord—
Pitying my love, if too superb to care
For hate-soiled name—an answer to my prayer.

VII

To me, who, vine to stone, clung close to thee,
  The very base of life appeared to quake
When first I knew thee fallen from us, to be
  A tower of strength among our foes, to make
'Twixt Jew and Jew deep-cloven enmity.
  I have wept gall and blood for thy dear sake.
But now with temperate soul I calmly search
Motive and cause that bound thee to the Church.

VIII

Four motives possible therefore I reach—
  Ambition, doubt, fear, or mayhap—conviction.
I hear in turn ascribed thee all and each
  By ignorant folk who part not truth from fiction.
But I, whom even thyself didst stoop to teach,
  May poise the scales, weigh this with that confliction,
Yea, sift the hid grain motive from the dense,
Dusty, eye-blinding chaff of consequence.

XIX

For some (I write it with flushed cheek, bowed head),
  Given free choice 'twixt death or shame, chose shame,
Denied the God who visibly had led
  Their fathers, pillared in a cloud of flame,
Bathed in baptismal waters, ate the bread
  Which is their new Lord's body, took the name
Marranos the Accursed, whom equally
Jew, Moor, and Christian hate, despise, and flee.

XX

Even one no less than an Abarbanel
  Prized miserable length of days, above
Integrity of soul. Midst such who fell,
  Far be it, however, from my duteous love,

Master, to reckon thee. Thine own lips tell
  How fear nor torture thy firm will could move.
How thou midst panic nowise disconcerted,
  By Thomas of Aquinas wast converted!

XXI

Truly I know no more convincing way
  To read so wise an author, than was thine.
When burning Synagogues changed night to day,
  And red swords underscored each word and line.
That was a light to read by! Who'd gainsay
  Authority so clearly stamped divine?
On this side, death and torture, flame and slaughter,
On that, a harmless wafer and clean water.

XXV

Where are the signs fulfilled whereby all men
  Should know the Christ? Where is the wide-winged peace
Shielding the lamb within the lion's den?
  The freedom broadening with the wars that cease?
Do foes clasp hands in brotherhood again?
  Where is the promised garden of increase,
When like a rose the wilderness should bloom?
Earth is a battlefield and Spain a tomb.

XXIV

Help me, O thou who wast my boyhood's guide,
  I bend my exile-weary feet to thee,
Teach me the indivisible to divide,
  Show me how three are one and One is three!
How Christ to save all men was crucified,
  Yet I and mine are damned eternally.
Instruct me, Sage, why Virtue starves alone,
While falsehood step by step ascends the throne.

Emma decided to send the poem to a Jewish magazine.
She thought of another work of hers that the editors of the
American Hebrew might be interested in publishing. "A few
years ago," she said in her letter, "I wrote a play founded on
an incident of medieval persecution of the Jews in Germany,
which I think it would be highly desirable to publish now, in
order to arouse sympathy and to emphasize the cruelty of the
injustice done to our unhappy people. . . ."

Her letter continued: "I write to ask if the American Hebrew Publishing Company will undertake to print it in pamphlet form." (For, she felt, it should not be issued as the typical volume of verse, slim and elegant—and expensive. It should be made available to the widest possible audience.)

She came back to her original reason for writing this letter—the "Epistle of Joshua Ibn Vives."

"I send you also a poem which I should be glad to have you publish, if you can make room for it. Will you kindly return it if you do not care for it? It has a strong bearing on the question of the day, besides having a curious historical interest.

"An early answer will greatly oblige me."

Philip Cowen, editor of the *American Hebrew*, was indeed interested in the work she submitted. He made arrangements to print both the "Epistle" and her play, *The Dance to Death*. Because of the drama's length, the magazine published it in installments. The first section appeared with a dedication to George Eliot, whose novel *Daniel Deronda* expressed such compassion and sympathy for the Jews—going so far as to herald a future national homeland for them in Palestine. Emma's tribute read:

This play is dedicated
IN PROFOUND VENERATION AND RESPECT
to the memory of
GEORGE ELIOT
the illustrious writer,
who did most among the artists of our day
towards elevating and ennobling
the spirit of Jewish nationality.

Cowen was excited that a poet of Emma Lazarus' stature was now offering her writings directly to a Jewish audience. His magazine had, in former years, reprinted some of her poems on Jewish themes from *Lippincott's*, the *Century*, and the *Critic*, and her translations from Heine.

He called upon her, suggesting that she write as often as possible for the *American Hebrew.* Emma took up his invitation eagerly.

Two weeks later, she sent him an editorial appealing for aid to the Russian-Jewish refugees and enclosed a note of inquiry. "Can you publish the accompanying little communication in this week's issue of your paper? Of course it must appear *anonymously*—and I beg to request particularly that *you do not divulge to anyone its authorship.*"

This request for anonymity was to crop up again and again. Was it extreme modesty, a hesitancy to face the world directly? Although this has been intimated, it seems unlikely, for Emma was willing to take full responsibility for the boldest of her writings. It would seem more plausible that she was conscious of the restrictions upon her sex at that time—women were not newspaper men, and certainly not a woman from a family background like hers. Besides, many people felt that poets could not deal with practical affairs. At any rate, Emma decided that her appeal would be more effective without any burden of other associations.

She wanted to help the refugees with all her heart, all her mind. Resources of money were not enough. Besides, how long could such aid be continued? To find homes and work for them were the two best ways to help.

For centuries, the Jews of Europe had been forbidden to own land or to plough the soil. Nevertheless, Emma was certain that they could be trained to become farmers. Had not the Jews been farmers in Israel? Were not the Jewish festivals of the New Year and of Succoth farmer's festivals?

She became interested in the efforts of the Hebrew Emigrant Aid Society to set up an agricultural colony in Vineland, New Jersey. Her deep enthusiasm was not without its lighter side. She wrote to Philip Cowen: "I see a note in your editorial column, suggesting the name of Washington for the Vineland colony. Please *don't publish this as coming from me,* but I hope in the name of common-sense and in compassion for the United

States Postmasters, that not one more addition to the American villages or settlements of any kind, by the name of Washington will be made! Every State has already an indefinite number of them causing much confusion and unnecessary bewilderment. Why not, if a name must be found, select that of some friend to the Jewish cause—such as *Eliot,* after George Eliot who had such a noble and eloquent sympathy with us—or some distinguished Jew—such as *Montefiore,* a beautiful name in itself."

But "anything," Emma urged, "rather than Washington, Lincoln, Jefferson or Garfield!"

She was ready to offer other suggestions. They could name the colony after another Moses—Moses Mendelssohn who, in the eighteenth century, led the Jewish emancipation movement in Germany. Or Beaconsfield—after Benjamin Disraeli, the Earl of Beaconsfield and Prime Minister of Great Britain; his would make a pleasant-sounding name. Or Abarbanel, in honor of Isaac Abarbanel, the Portuguese Jew, treasurer to King Ferdinand and Queen Isabella of Spain, who joined the Jewish exodus when they expelled his people in 1492.

Emma wrote a sonnet recalling that "two-faced year" when the Jews were cast out from their Spanish homeland, and when Columbus voyaged to the New World where all would be free:

1492

Thou two-faced year, Mother of Change and Fate,
Didst weep when Spain cast forth with flaming sword,
The children of the prophets of the Lord,
Prince, priest, and people, spurned by zealot hate.
Hounded from sea to sea, from state to state,
The West refused them, and the East abhorred.
No anchorage the known world could afford,
Close-locked was every port, barred every gate.
Then smiling, thou unveil'dst, O two-faced year,
A virgin world where doors of sunset part,
Saying, "Ho, all who weary, enter here!
There falls each ancient barrier that the art
Of race or creed or rank devised, to rear
Grim bulwarked hatred between heart and heart!

She sought to give the refugees strength by recalling their heritage. Because of that rich heritage, the Jews had endured throughout the ages; reminded of it anew, they could survive the present difficulties. The perpetual lamp, the light of truth and justice, had been handed down from generation unto generation; let her people now hold fast to its radiance. Such was her message in another poem written in 1883, in which she portrayed four differing ways of life among four ancient peoples:

GIFTS

"O World-God, give me Wealth!" the Egyptian cried.
His prayer was granted. High as heaven, behold
Palace and Pyramid; the brimming tide
Of lavish Nile washed all his land with gold.
Armies of slaves toiled ant-wise at his feet,
World-circling traffic roared through mart and street,
His priests were gods, his spice-balmed kings enshrined,
Set death at naught in rock-ribbed charnels deep.
Seek Pharaoh's race today and ye shall find
Rust and the moth, silence and dusty sleep.

"O World-God, give me Beauty!" cried the Greek.
His prayer was granted. All the world became
Plastic and vocal to his sense; each peak,
Each groove, each stream, quick with Promethean flame,
Peopled the world with imaged grace and light.
The lyre was his, and his the breathing might
Of the immortal marble, his the play
Of diamond-pointed thought and golden tongue.
Go seek the sun-shine race, ye shall find today
A broken column and a lute unstrung.

"O World-God, give me Power!" the Roman cried.
His prayer was granted. The vast world was chained
A captive to the chariot of his pride.
The blood of myriad provinces was drained
To feed that fierce, insatiable red heart.
Invulnerably bulwarked every part
With serried legions and with close-meshed code.
Within, the burrowing worm had gnawed its home,
A roofless ruin stands where once abode
The imperial race of everlasting Rome.

"O Godhead, give me Truth!" the Hebrew cried.
His prayer was granted; he became the slave
Of the Idea, a pilgrim far and wide,
Cursed, hated, spurned, and scourged with none to save.
The Pharaohs knew him, and when Greece beheld,
His wisdom wore the hoary crown of Eld.
Beauty he hath forsworn, and wealth and power.
Seek him today, and find in every land.
No fire consumes him, neither floods devour;
Immortal through the lamp within his hand.

America, Emma felt, broad-spanning in its democracy, would continue to be the New World of freedom and tolerance for the Jews. She felt like weeping for sheer joy when Michael Heilprin showed her a letter from a Jewish refugee now resettled in Texas.

From their trials in the Old World, he and a group of his townsmen had come upon fresh troubles in America. First settling in Louisiana, they had been flooded off the land they had settled on. Going on to the Midwest, they had been burnt out by drought. Finally, in fertile Texas, "our life is one unbroken paradise. We live a true brotherly life. Every evening after supper we take a seat under the mighty oak and sing our songs."

Emma felt impelled to answer song with song. Quoting from the letter, she wrote "In Exile":

Twilight is here, soft breezes bow the grass,
Day's sounds of various toil break slowly off,
The yoke-freed oxen low, the patient ass
Dips his dry nostril in the cool, deep trough.
Up from the prairie the tanned herdsmen pass
With frothy pails, guiding with voices rough
Their udder-lightened kine. Fresh smells of earth,
The rich, black furrows of the glebe send forth.

After the Southern day of heavy toil,
How good to lie, with limbs relaxed, brows bare
To evening's fan, and watch the smoke-wreaths coil
Up from one's pipe-stem through the rayless air.
So deem these unused tillers of the soil,
Who stretched beneath the shadowing oak-tree, stare
Peacefully on the star-unfolding skies,
And name their life unbroken paradise.

The hounded stag that has escaped the pack,
  And pants at ease within a thick-leaved dell;
The unimprisoned bird that finds the track
  Through sun-bathed space, to where his fellows dwell;
The martyr, granted respite from the rack,
  The death-doomed victim pardoned from his cell—
Such only know the joy these exiles gain,—
Life's sharpest rapture is surcease of pain.

Strange faces theirs, where through the Orient sun
  Gleams from the eyes and glows athwart the skin.
Grave lines of studious thought and purpose run
  From curl-crowned forehead to dark-bearded chin.
And over all the seal is stamped thereon
  Of anguish branded by a world of sin,
In fire and blood through ages on their name,
Their seal of glory and the Gentiles' shame.

Freedom to love the law that Moses brought,
  To sing the songs of David, and to think
The thoughts Gabirol to Spinoza taught,
  Freedom to dig the common earth, to drink
The universal air—for this they sought
  Refuge o'er wave and continent, to link
Egypt with Texas in their mystic chain,
And truth's perpetual lamp forbid to wane.

Hark! through the quiet evening air, their song
  Floats forth with wild sweet rhythm and glad refrain.
They sing the conquest of the spirit strong,
  The soul that wrests the victory from pain;
The noble joys of manhood that belong
  To comrades and to brothers. In their strain
Rustle of palms and Eastern streams one hears,
And the broad prairie melts in mist of tears.

How proud she had become of her Jewish heritage! The American Hebrew Publishing Company was about to issue her *The Dance to Death* in permanent book-form after its magazine appearance; her newly written poems would also be included. Emma wrote to Cowen, reminding him again of her desire for pamphlet publication: "It is my idea to have the pamphlet issued at as low a price and in as simple a form as possible."

Cowen acceded to her wish. There would be no expensive edition, no gold-stamped, leather-bound volume for the elite. A cloth edition would be produced to sell for fifty cents; the paper-bound pamphlet for twenty-five cents, to make it available to the widest possible audience.

Emma mulled over a title. It should be bold, outspoken. These were poems on Jewish themes by a Jewish poet. Let it be clearly understood. She would call it *Songs of a Semite*.

8

THE PROUD NAME OF JEW

🌷 By September, the *American Hebrew* was displaying advertisements for the forthcoming volume, "printed on fine, tinted paper, from large, clear type. Price, in paper, 25 cents . . . in cloth, 50 cents."

The price was unprecedented, but Emma had become a confirmed rule-breaker! Emma now asked them to hold the press a little longer. So driving was her creative urge, that almost every day she was writing new poems: poems for her people, that must be included in the pamphlet.

As a publisher, with the presses ready to roll, Philip Cowen was impatient; as an editor, after reading the poems, he agreed with her. Especially would he wait for lines such as these from "The Crowing of the Red Cock":

> Across the Eastern sky has glowed
>   The flicker of a blood-red dawn,
> Once more the clarion cock has crowed,
>   Once more the sword of Christ is drawn.
> A million burning rooftrees light
> The world-wide path of Israel's flight.
>
> Where is the Hebrew's fatherland?
>   The folk of Christ is sore bestead;
> The Son of Man is bruised and banned,
>   Nor finds whereon to lay his head.
> His cup is gall, his meat is tears,
> His passion lasts a thousand years.
>
> Each crime that wakes in man the beast,
>   Is visited upon his kind.
> The lust of mobs, the greed of priest,
>   The tyranny of kings, combined

To root his seed from earth again,
His record is one cry of pain.

When the long roll of Christian guilt
   Against his sires and kin is known,
The flood of tears, the life-blood spilt,
   The agony of ages shown,
What oceans can the stain remove,
From Christian law and Christian love?

Nay, close the book; not now, not here,
   The hideous tale of sin narrate,
Reechoing in the martyr's ear,
   Even he might nurse revengeful hate,
Even he might turn in wrath sublime,
With blood for blood and crime for crime.

Coward? Not he, who faces death,
   Who singly against worlds has fought,
For what? A name he may not breathe,
   For liberty of prayer and thought.
The angry sword he will not whet
His nobler task is—to forget.

Songs of a Semite was received with acclaim by critics here
and abroad, by Jewish readers and by non-Jews alike. *The
Dance to Death* was seen as an historical drama of great power,
made even more significant by the current Tsarist persecution
of the Jews. Her shorter lyrics and the translations from Hebrew
poets (despite the handicap of having to work from German
versions) were widely appreciated. John Greenleaf Whittier said
that "since Miriam sang of deliverance and triumph by the Red
Sea, the Semitic race has had no braver singer. 'The Crowing
Of The Red Cock,' written when the Russian sky was red with
blazing Hebrew homes, is an indignant and forceful lyric worthy
of the Maccabean age."
    Gratified at the reception of her pamphlet, Emma, neverthe-
less, shrank from personal publicity. When she heard about an
elaborate advertising sign announcing forthcoming features in
the *American Hebrew* with her own name spelled out in lights,

she dashed off a sharp note of protest to Philip Cowen. "If you have any knowledge or connection with this advertisement, I request that it be discontinued forthwith. I cannot understand how you could adopt this rather peculiar mode of advertising, without first consulting my wishes in the matter, and shall await impatiently for assurance that a stop has been put to it."

Shy, yet forthright. Also, in the detection of hidden anti-Semitism, as when praise was combined with suspicious criticism from Samuel Gray Ward. "Perhaps you are right," Emma replied, "about the 'range of the medieval Hebrew poets being too limited to awaken general interest'—but I must beg you to remember that the specimens I have translated are taken at random, and bear no relation whatever to the immense treasury of poetry that lies hidden in its original source. The three poets represented in my little collection have each a marked individuality, and have by no means confined themselves to strictly religious poetry. I am studying Hebrew, and hope soon to be able to appreciate them in the original. Then I shall be more competent to weigh the worth of your objection."

With her flair for languages, the mastery of Hebrew came quickly. In a matter of months, she was able to translate directly from the source. How indebted she felt to her friend, Rabbi Gottheil, who had opened to her the rich treasure-house of ancient Hebrew poetry! Rabbi Gottheil also helped her to understand and appreciate the wealth of other writings of the past— he deepened her knowledge of Jewish ideals as they were outlined in the Mosaic code, in Jewish lore and living.

Frequently, another dear friend, Michael Heilprin, accompanied her on her visits to the refugees on Ward's Island. The Schiff Refuge there, named after the donor, and the Hebrew Emigrant Aid Society shelter were swamped. They were of flimsy construction, and Heilprin pointed out that they would provide adequate shelter during the warm months but would afford cold comfort when winter came. Conditions inside the buildings were even worse.

Emma wrote a letter to the *American Hebrew*, protesting the housing, the poor food, and the uncleanliness. ". . . The only appliances for washing consist of about a dozen tubs in the laundry and ten bath-tubs in the lavatory." (This, for seven hundred people!) "Not a drop of running water is to be found in dormitories or refectories, or in any of the other buildings, except the kitchen. In all weathers, those who desire to wash their hands or to fetch a cup of water, have to walk over several hundred feet of irregular, dirty ground, strewn with rubbish and refuse, and filled, after a rainfall, with stagnant pools of muddy water in which throngs of idle children are allowed to dabble at will. . . ."

From concrete suggestions for improving the physical quarters, she went on to what she considered the greatest need of all— useful work that would restore the dignity of life.

After finishing her letter, she jotted down ideas for future activity: "Upon every Jewish school and asylum in the land, religious or secular, should be grafted a system of instruction in some branch of productive industry." And it was the solemn duty of American Jewry "to foster a spirit of union and nationality, and at the same time to reform the internal abuses of our present social condition."

One afternoon, Philip Cowen walked uptown to the Lazarus house. He had asked Emma to write a special poem; she had refused, but he wanted to talk to her further about it.

Emma came to the front door to welcome him in. At the same time, her pretty younger sister, Annie, entered. Annie was dressed in the height of fashion, her gloved hand resting delicately on the arm of an equally well dressed youth. Cowen recognized him as one of the sons of the noted publisher, Charles Dana.

As they passed inside, Cowen flushed. Annie's clear, though

hushed voice was explaining: "Oh, he's Emma's *Jewish* editor . . ."

Cowen turned to Emma, studied her face for some sign, some clue. She had either not heard, or was deliberately ignoring the remark. She must surely have heard, he thought; she had a keen ear. Yet she continued their conversation as though nothing had occurred. "Now about my writing a poem to celebrate the Jewish New Year, as you were asking—"

"Yes. Oh yes, of course." What a remarkably fine person she was, Cowen noted, for perhaps the hundredth time. And then he sighed, and noted for the hundred and first time, what a remarkably complicated and paradoxical person she was!

For Emma went on: "I'm afraid I won't be able to do it for you. I can't do things to order, you know. I'm a poet, not a journalist."

Cowen shrugged. If she wouldn't, then she wouldn't. He knew how stubbornly determined she was; he wouldn't waste time arguing. But *wouldn't* did not mean that she *couldn't*— but of course since she didn't care to try, to test herself . . .

"No." Emma refused to take up the challenge.

Very well. But as Cowen took leave of her, he mentioned casually in what a beautiful season the Jewish New Year occurred. In autumn, at the height of Nature's splendor and bounty. (It was no secret to him that the fall had always been Emma's favorite season.) Didn't Miss Lazarus agree that it was a rich tradition for the Jews to initiate their New Year at the harvest time, instead of in bleak midwinter? Well, it was only a passing thought. Cowen picked up his hat.

The next day, going over his mail, he smiled as he recognized Emma's handwriting. He had been right; she couldn't resist the theme!

In Emma's majestic lines there was nothing of austerity. This was a joyous, a triumphant celebration:

THE NEW YEAR

Rosh-Hashanah, 5643 (1882)

Not while the snow-shroud round dead earth is rolled,
And naked branches point to frozen skies;
When orchards burn their lamps of fiery gold,
The grape glows like a jewel, and the corn
A sea of beauty and abundance lies,
    Then the new year is born.

Look where the mother of the months uplifts
    In the green clearness of the unsunned West,
Her ivory horn of plenty, dropping gifts,
    Cool, harvest-feeding dews, fine-winnowed light;
Tired labor with fruition, joy and rest
    Profusely to requite.

Blow, Israel, the sacred cornet! Call
    Back to thy courts whatever faint heart throbs
With thine ancestral blood, thy need craves all.
The red, dark year is dead, the year just born
Leads on from anguish wrought by priest and mob,
    To what undreamed-of morn?

For never yet, since on the holy height,
    The Temple's marble walls of white and green
Carved like the sea-waves, fell, and the world's light
    Went out in darkness,—never was the year
Greater with portent and with promise seen,
    Than this eve now and here.

Even as the Prophet promised, so your tent
    Hath been enlarged unto earth's farthest rim.
To snow-capped Sierras from vast steppes ye went,
    Through fire and blood and tempest-tossing wave,
For freedom to proclaim and worship Him,
    Mighty to slay and save.

High above flood and fire ye held the scroll,
    Out of the depths ye published still the Word.
No bodily pang has power to swerve your soul:
    Ye, in a cynic age of crumbling faiths,
Lived to bear witness to the living Lord,
    Or died a thousand deaths.

In two divided streams the exiles part,
One rolling homeward to its ancient source,
One rushing sunward with fresh will, new heart.
By each the truth is spread, the law unfurled,
Each separate soul contains the nation's force,
And both embrace the world.

Kindle the silver candle's seven rays,
Offer the first fruits of the clustered bowers,
The garnered spoil of bees. With prayer and praise
Rejoice that once more tried, once more we prove
How strength of supreme suffering still is ours
For Truth and Law and Love.

She had so many ideas, so much she wanted to say! Poems could not contain it all; she required debate, argument, an airing of discussion.

To communicate her message, since she shrank from public speaking, she conceived of "An Epistle to the Hebrews."

To the many requests that had come to her to deliver lectures or read her poems, she had given the same reply: "I beg to say that anything in the nature of a lecture or an address is entirely beyond my province and capacity." Almost invariably she would add, however, that she would write the address asked for, for someone else to read. We can detect the implication that someday, if she were pressed hard enough, she might consent.

Emma Lazarus was—as we all are—a product of the age. In that age a "well brought-up" woman shrank from making a public appearance. Had she been born Eliezer or Ezra rather than Emma . . .

Instead she wrote her great *"Epistle to the Hebrews,"* ranging wide and deep, criticizing, exhorting, guiding. It took sixteen weekly installments in the *American Hebrew,* from November 1882 to February 1883. It was an almost unparalleled streak of creative energy.

She wanted above all to give her people pride. They must not cringe or hide the name of Jew. "Tell a man he is brave, and you help him to become so," Thomas Carlyle had said. And the reverse was equally true, Emma felt. "Our adversaries are perpetually throwing dust in our eyes," she wrote, "with accusations of materialism and tribalism, and we in our pitiable endeavor to conform to the required standard, plead guilty and fall into the trap they set. That our national temper and character have suffered grievous injury during our thousand-year-long struggle for existence is undeniable, but the injury has been precisely of an opposite nature to that which the world would have us believe. It has been a physical and material loss, as well as a loss of that homogeneity and united national sentiment which it is our first duty to revive in order to concentrate our efforts towards regeneration and rehabilitation. 'Tribal!' This perpetual taunt rings so persistently in our ears that most Jews themselves are willing to admit its justice, in the face of the fact that our 'tribal God' has become the God of two-thirds of the inhabited globe, the God of Islam and of Christendom, and that as a people we have adapted ourselves to the varying customs and climates of every nation in the world.

"In defiance of the hostile construction that may be put upon my words, I do not hesitate to say that our national defect is that we are not 'tribal' enough; we have not sufficient solidarity to perceive that when the life and property of a Jew in the uttermost provinces of the Caucasus are attacked, the dignity of a Jew in free America is humiliated.

"We who are prosperous and independent have not sufficient homogeneity to champion on the ground of a common creed, common stock, a common history, a common heritage of misfortune, the rights of the lowest and poorest Jew peddler who flees, for life and liberty of thought, from Slavonic mobs. Until we are all free, we are none of us free.

"But lest we should justify the taunts of our opponents, lest we should become 'tribal' and narrow and Judaic rather than humane and cosmopolitan like the anti-Semites of Germany and the Jew-baiters of Russia, we ignore and repudiate our

unhappy brethren as having no part or share in their misfortunes
—until the cup of anguish is held also to our own lips. . . ."

Emma's voice, through the words of her open letter, rang
out in scorn. With the range of a virtuoso, she could change
her style, make every note in the scale resound—from compassion, to sarcasm, to pleading. She revived the past, dreamed
of the future—and insisted on the present as a practical bridge
spanning the way.

"What we need today second only to the necessity of closer
union and warmer patriotism," she demanded, "is the building
up of our national, physical force. If the new Ezra arose to
lead our people to a secure house of refuge, whence would he
recruit the farmers, masons, carpenters, artisans, competent to
perform the arduous practical pioneer work of founding a new
nation? We read of the Jews who attempted to rebuild the
Temple using the trowel with one hand, while with the other
they warded off the blows of the molesting enemy. Where are
the warrior-mechanics of today equal to either feat?"

Jews, she argued, could and should do many kinds of work
—including manual labor, and farming.

Another axiom set her off on a new installment of her
Epistle. ". . . 'It is always the impossible which happens,' said
a witty Frenchman, and the axiom is applicable in a peculiar
sense to the Jewish people. 'A Jew may be a prophet, but cannot
be a philosopher,' the world once fancied, and the Jews produced a Philo, a Maimonides, a Spinoza. After we had been
for centuries excluded from political life, we were told that a
Jew could not be a statesman. But the external barriers were
removed, and within a single generation behold a Disraeli, a
Lasker [a German leader who helped bring about the unifica-
tion of Germany], a Gambetta [French Radical deputy and
premier]. . . . And now, as if the greater did not include the
less, we hear on all sides the cry, 'A Jew cannot be an agri-
culturist.'

"Read the reports of the colonies of refugees at Cotopaxi, Colorado, and Vineland, New Jersey, and you have facts and figures as a victorious declaration of the truth that the Hebrew can be a farmer and is a farmer. The *Jewish Chronicle* tells us that 'at Piedmont there has lately been held an Industrial, and at Turin an Agricultural Exhibition. In both places Jews gained prizes.' "

She summed up her argument: "Antipathy to manual labor is one of the great social diseases of our age and country." That antipathy had to be overcome, else the people could not go forward. She called upon the wisdom of past ages. "The Talmud says: 'Get your living by skinning carcasses in the street if you cannot otherwise; and do not say, I am a priest, I am a great man, this work would not befit my dignity.'

". . . Jewish schools and colleges such as the famous intellectual seats of Babylon, flourished in the midst of what has been aptly called a 'mental wilderness.' But cheering as this picture is, it has still another bright side which is not sufficiently taken into account. 'These youths and men who attended the schools,' says the eminent Talmudist, Dr. Jastrow, 'were *farmers, mechanics, tradesmen,* none of them taking up learning as a means of support, or to speak Talmudically as a "spade to dig with" . . . Jewish farmers devoting their leisure hours to study, Jewish youths and men twice a year, *when their agricultural pursuits would allow them a vacation,* streamed to the centres of learning.' This is the feature of our past upon which it behooves us to insist at present . . ."

She wrote rapidly, almost with the quickness of conversation. She cajoled, buttonholed, pointed the finger of scorn and indignation, held out her arms in sympathy.

"The unworthy desire on the part of many Jews to conceal their lineage, evinced in the constant transmutation of family-names, and in the contemptible aversion and hostility manifested between Jews of varying descent, painfully prove the

absence of both the spirit and training essential to a higher
national existence. . . . If I speak with occasional severity of the
weakness or the degeneracy in certain points of my people, I
premise that I do so with full appreciation of the heroic martyrdom of ages that has in great part engendered their national
defects. Not for the sake of those who have mainly begotten in
us the faults inseparable from long subjection to oppression and
contempt, but for our own sakes, for the sake of the coming
generation, I shall endeavor to impress upon my readers the
urgent necessity for reform along the whole line of Jewish
thought and Jewish life, and for a deepening and quickening
of the sources of Jewish enthusiasm . . .

". . . To the early Greek the world was divided into
Greeks and Barbarians; the primitive Jew saw only 'strangers,'
blasphemers and idolators in the nations that surrounded him.
But when the Greeks were themselves swallowed up by the
Barbarians, and the chief city of Hellenistic thought was no
longer Athens but Rome, the pagan poet formulated the immortal axiom: 'I am a Man, and nothing that is human can
be alien to me.'

"Similarly when the Jews who had hitherto been acquainted
only with intellectually inferior nations, suddenly found themselves face to face in Alexandria with the race that had invented
philosophy and art, then they too awoke to the fact that good
existed outside of Judaism, and without abandoning their own
intellectual stronghold, they proved as usual swift and prompt
to assimilate all that was desirable in the surrounding civilization . . .

"From this time onward, the accusation of a narrow tribalism
can never be made with justice against Judaism; it has imbibed
and thoroughly assimilated the broad notion of a common humanity, by the light of which it interprets into a new significance
the teachings of the older Prophets. . . .

"To combine the conservation of one's own individuality

with a due respect for the rights of every other individuality, is the ideal condition of society, but it is a foolish perversion of this truth to deduce therefrom the obligation to renounce all individuality and this remark is no less applicable to nations than to persons.

"Not by disclaiming our 'full heritage,' but by lifting up our own race to the standard of morality and instruction shall we at the same time promote the advancement and elevation of the Gentiles. . . . To carry out this exalted conception we require a nation of priests, that is to say, of priests in the best and original sense of the word—devoted servants of the Holy Spirit. But if our people persist in entrenching themselves behind a Chinese wall of petrified religious forms, the great modern stream of scientific philosophy will sweep past them, carrying Humanity to new heights, and will leave them far in the rear. The question is, where are we to look in America for the patriotic Jew whose intellect is sufficiently expanded to accept all the conclusions of science, and yet whose sense of the moral responsibilities and glories bequeathed to him by his ancestors is sufficiently vivid to kindle him into a missionary and a prophet?"

Her fingers were cramped from writing, her head ached with fatigue, yet she was reluctant to stop. There was so much to think about, to write!

With the objectivity of a writer observing herself as well as the world, she smiled at her sense of urgency. These problems had existed for thousands of years, and she had the temerity to think she could contribute towards a solution! And yet, why not? She was a woman, she was a Jew, she was an American, and her concern was "the oppression of men and women by men and women."

She would shake the complacent off their couches, to go to the aid of their barefoot, beggared brothers and sisters . . . So she appealed with all her heart: "It will be a lasting blot upon American Judaism—nay, upon *prosperous* Judaism of whatever nationality—if we do not come forward now with encouragement for the disheartened and help for the helpless, or if we neglect this opportunity to dignify our race and our name by vigorous, united and disinterested action.

"To fail in such an attempt is no disgrace—the disgrace is in not undertaking it.

"Our own position of security places any efforts we make in this direction beyond the imputation of personal or unworthy motives. Our comparative remoteness from the scene of agitation enables us to judge oppressor and oppressed almost with the calmness of posterity. Our national American unconcern in the complicated entanglements of European politics gives us a peculiar clearness of vision and coolness of head wherewith to measure the chances and advantages of international alliances. We possess the double cosmopolitanism of the American and the Jew. We see the leashed and greedy hounds of European power straining at their checks, ready to pounce upon the tempting morsel of Egyptian supremacy, or struggling to be freed for the chase and to be 'in at the death' of the Ottoman Empire. We have only to watch and wait, and to put ourselves in readiness for action upon an emergency. 'The gods themselves,' says a Chinese proverb, 'cannot help him who loses opportunities.' "

The opportunity was here. The pressing weight of injustice was felt; she wanted to help lift it with her strength and knowledge, her creative powers, and to exhort others to share in the task. What had been history was now as immediate and urgent as today's headlines. She could not afford the isolation of "pure poetry"; she had to become a journalist, a reporter of life.

She brought the manuscript of her latest installment of the *Epistle* to Philip Cowen, as he stood at the roaring presses. He held up his hands to show the ink stains. Not wanting to stain her manuscript pages, he motioned her to the front office.

But Emma lingered; she liked the smell of the presses, the

metal, the lead, the ink, and the roar of machinery. This had its own freshness and music, the smells and sounds of work. Ignoring the grime, she walked from one machine to another. Out of all this confusion and clatter would come order—words set into the harmony of print for people to read and act upon.

9

INNER CONFLICTS

❦ In her studies, in conversations with people like Philip Cowen and Michael Heilprin, in meeting with committees to raise funds for the needy refugees and help find work for them, in all that she now did, Emma's mind ranged over a multitude of questions.

Several years before, Emma had become interested in the work of Henry George. The American economist and social reformer had published his book *Progress and Poverty* in 1879. Disturbed by the greatly uneven relationships between the rich and the poor, George suggested that one of the ways to adjust such inequality would be to impose a single tax—a tax on land. "We hold," George wrote, "that to tax land values to their full amount will render it impossible for any man to exact from others a price for the privilege of using those bounties."

He added, ". . . it will provide opportunities of work for all men and secure to each the full reward of his labor; and . . . as a result involuntary poverty will be abolished, and the greed, intemperance and vice that spring from poverty will be swept away."

George's book was widely read and discussed; within a short time it was translated into a dozen different languages. His followers organized "single-tax" clubs to promote the idea.

Emma was stirred by George's vision and wrote a sonnet in tribute to his book. In the fall of 1881 the *New York Times* published her poem.

PROGRESS AND POVERTY

(*After Reading Mr. Henry George's Book*)

Oh splendid age when Science lights her lamp
At the brief lightning's momentary flame,
Fixing it steadfast as a star, man's name
Upon the very brow of heaven to stamp!
Launched on a ship whose iron-cuirassed sides
Mock storm and wave, Humanity sails free;
Gayly upon a vast, untraveled sea,
O'er pathless wastes, to ports undreamed she rides,
Richer than Cleopatra's barge of gold,
This vessel, manned by demi-gods, with freight
Of priceless marvels. But where yawns the hold
In that deep reeking hell, what slaves be they,
Who feed the ravenous monster, pant and sweat,
Nor know if overhead reign night or day?

Her image for Progress is well-chosen; in the ship we have
a feeling of forward motion. She goes on to give us a sharply
contrasting picture of life above and below deck. The language
is clear and bold; she does not substitute Hades for *hell*. Her
use of the word *sweat* was extremely daring for that time when
"only horses sweat—men perspire and ladies glow." Her use
of the word is no accidental search for a rhyme, for it is the
only word in the entire sonnet scheme that does not rhyme! And
she could easily have found the rhyme that was required by conventional standards: *wait, Fate, late, state, create:* the possibili-
ties are many. Obviously, her use of the unconventional word
was deliberate.

Emma sent George a copy of her poem and he replied promptly
and graciously, enclosing a recent pamphlet of his on economics.
His letter expressed to Emma "the gratification of feeling that
one of your gifts hears that appeal that once heard can never
be forgotten."

Writing in return to thank him for the pamphlet, Emma
said: "I wish I could convey to you an idea of the feelings
aroused in me by your book. No thinking man or woman in

these days can have remained altogether deaf to that mute
'appeal which once heard can never be forgotten'. But the same
appeal when interpreted by your burning eloquence takes possession of one's mind and heart to such a degree as overpowers
all other voices. Your work is not so much a book as an event
—the life and thought of no one capable of understanding it
can be quite the same after reading it—and even in the small
circle of my personal friends I have had abundant evidence of
the manner in which it sets the minds of men on fire—'all
men capable of feeling the inspiration of a great principle.' And
how should it be otherwise? For once prove the indisputable
truth of your ideas, and no person who prizes justice or common
honesty can dine or sleep or read or work in peace until the
monstrous wrong in which we are all accomplices be done away
with. I congratulate you most heartily on the natural gifts with
which you have been endowed for the noble cause you have
espoused. Great as is the idea, it would certainly fail to kindle
men's minds as it does now, if pleaded with less passionate
eloquence, by less authoritative knowledge.

"I am glad to hear that your stay abroad is to be a short
one, for I shall allow myself the pleasure of looking forward
confidently to the hope of seeing you on your return. We have
many mutual friends—but I am proud to think that I need not
rely upon any one else to bring us together. We have spoken
with each other and know each other's voices, and at the end
of six months or six years, if I were still here, I should be no
less sure of your sympathy and friendly remembrance. Mean-
time with earnest wishes for yourself and your cause, believe me,
                    Gratefully and sincerely yours,
                          Emma Lazarus."

Years later a message from Henry George troubled her. "I
did not propose to you," he said, "to write songs for *your*
people, but for *the* people."

She was startled. The Jewish cause, she felt, was wide and deep, ranging over many areas, crossing many boundaries of beliefs. But was she so absorbed, so caught up in its core, its center, that she could not see beyond?

Emma sought within herself and her studies for the answer. Finally, she felt justified in replying to George. In writing for her own, she was addressing herself to all the peoples of the world. For were not the foundations of truth, of justice, laid down in the Mosaic Code?

But George's prodding required a longer, more thoughtful response. Her opinions were not changed. She felt the truth and weight of her argument, that the Jewish cause concerned Jews and non-Jews alike. But she must reach out for a wider audience. If George felt as he did, there must be many more whom she needed to convince.

She would continue with her *Epistle* in the weekly pages of the *American Hebrew,* but she would also open her ideas to a general audience, to broader discussion. There was the *Century* magazine, devoted to the arts and topics of the day. She would use its pages to make clear that the Jewish cause concerned the whole thoughtful world.

"The Jewish problem," her article began, "is as old as history, and assumes in each age a new form. The life or death of millions of human beings hangs upon its solution; its agitation revives the fiercest passions for good and for evil that inflame the human breast. From the era when the monotheistic, Semitic slaves of the Pharaohs made themselves hated and feared by their polytheistic masters, till today when the monstrous giants Labor and Capital are arming for a supreme conflict, the Jewish question has been inextricably bound up with the deepest and gravest questions that convulse society . . .

"Even in America, presumably the refuge of the oppressed, public opinion has not yet reached that point where it absolves the race from the sin of the individual. Every Jew, however

honorable or enlightened, has the humiliating knowledge that
his security and reputation are, in a certain sense, bound up
with those of the meanest rascal who belongs to his tribe, and
who has it in his power to jeopardize the social status of his
whole nation.

"It has been well said that the Jew must be of gold in order
to pass for silver.

"Since the establishment of the American Union, Jews have
here enjoyed absolute civil and political freedom and equality,
and until the past few years, a large and in some places almost
entire immunity from social prejudice. . . .

"And yet here, too, the everlasting prejudice is cropping out
in various shapes. Within recent years, Jews have been 'boy-
cotted' at not a few places of public resort; in our schools and
colleges, even in our scientific universities, Jewish scholars are
frequently subjected to annoyance on account of their race. The
word 'Jew' is in constant use, even among so-called refined
Christians, as a term of opprobrium, and is employed as a verb,
to denote the meanest tricks.

"In other words, all the magnanimity, patience, charity, and
humanity, which the Jews have manifested in return for centuries
of persecution, have been thus far inadequate to eradicate the
profound antipathy engendered by fanaticism, and ready to
break out in one or another shape at any moment of popular
excitement. . . .''

This was hardly the polite kind of tea table talk one would
expect from a lady brought up in such sheltered society as Emma
Lazarus! But if superstition and ignorance were to be corrected,
one could not use delicately indirect language. One had to come
to the point. She continued:

"The insatiable thirst of the Jews is not for money, as
calumniously asserted, but for knowledge. In those districts of
Poland and Russia where they are refused admittance to the
schools, they have had books of natural science and Darwinian

treatises translated into Hebrew in order to follow the intellectual movement of the age. . . .

"It is assumed by Christian historians that the Jews, with their inflexible adherence to the Mosaic Code, are, as a people, a curious relic of remote antiquity, a social anachronism, so to speak—petrified in the midst of advancing civilization. This assumption is without foundation; the Jews are, on the contrary, most frequently the pioneers of progress. . . .

"The modern theory of socialism and humanitarianism, erroneously traced to the New Testament, has its root in the Mosaic Code. The Christian doctrine is the doctrine of consolation; the kingdom of heaven is held out as a glittering dream to suffering humanity. Poverty exalted into a mission, the vocation of the mystic, the spiritualist, the idealist, enjoyed equally upon all, a vision and an ecstasy offered to the hungry and the needy; what provision is here made for the world as it is?

"On the other hand, the very latest reforms urged by political economists, in view of the misery of the lower classes, are established by the Mosaic Code, which formulated the principle of the rights of labor, denying the right of private property in land, asserting that the corners of the field, the gleanings of the harvest belonged in *justice,* not in *charity,* to the poor and the stranger; and that man owed a duty, not only to all humanity, but even to the beast of the field, and 'the ox that treads the corn.' In accordance with these principles we find the fathers of modern socialism to be three Jews—Ferdinand Lassalle, Karl Marx, and Johann Jacoby. . . ."

Emma was indeed correct when she stated that the Jewish problem concerned Jews and non-Jews alike. Conservatives of every faith were shocked by her bold definitions of the rights of labor.

Many were even more horrified by her new ideas about the sacred Sabbath set forth in one of her weekly *Epistles.* Emma was exalting that holy day not as a day of piety and repentance, but of joy. She recalled what the Sabbath meant to the Jews in earlier times. "However degrading or servile might be their avocations during the secular week, the first star of the Sabbath eve restored to them their human dignity, when they met in the Synagogue or around the family board, however humble, to sing, in the midst of bondage and oppression, those Psalms which have been for all ages, the battle cry of freedom, and to cherish the memory of days when they were a nation of princes and priests. The Sabbath was distinguished from the weekday by holiday apparel, by convivial gatherings, by music and gayety; the only limit to these was the equal right of every individual to undisturbed rest from labor.

"Whoever pauses to consider how large a part of the pleasures of the rich depends upon the ceaseless toil of the poor, will see how great a proportion of daily amusement and luxury is cut off by this humane injunction. But such a restriction in modes of enjoyment, has nothing in common with the gloomy horrors of the Calvinistic Sunday, or the asceticism, the wearisome solemnity and repeated devotional exercises of the Puritans. Ours is the joyous spirit of the Roman Catholic Sabbath, with the simple difference that the humanity of the Jew never loses sight of the fact that in order to keep restaurants, theatres, concert and dancing-halls open on the day of rest, as in the gay Catholic towns of Continental Europe, thousands of men and women are deprived of one of the greatest privileges ever accorded by legislation to the poor. Amid the actual conditions of our complex civilization, it would be neither desirable nor possible to revive in full force the Jewish Sabbath which was adapted to the needs of a comparatively simple agricultural society. But if there be any question of such a revival, let us at least understand what the Jewish Sabbath is, and not confound it with the stern and unpoetical Sunday of the New England Puritans, or with the ludicrous injunctions of the New York Sunday Penal Code. . . ."

What a howl went up from the prim and the grim!

It is interesting to note that, although Emma Lazarus took no part in the organized movement for women's rights, often —as in this case—her ideas coincided with theirs. Elizabeth Cady Stanton, for example, one of the founders of the women's rights movement in this country, also demanded religious reformation and a more humane conception of Sunday.

Controversy over Emma's ideas swelled, spilled and spluttered over. What would she think of next? Now she was insisting that a national homeland be established for the Jews!

". . . The melancholy and disgraceful fact being established that, in these closing decades of the nineteenth century, the long-suffering Jew is still universally exposed to injustice, proportioned to the barbarity of the nation that surrounds him, from the indescribable atrocities of Russian mobs, through every degree of refined insult to petty mortification, the inevitable result has been to arouse most thinking Jews to the necessity of a vigorous and concerted action of defense. They have long enough practiced to no purpose the doctrine which Christendom has been content to preach, and which was inculcated by one of their own race— when the right cheek was smitten, to turn also the left. They have proved themselves willing and able to assimilate with whatever people and to endure every climatic influence. But blind intolerance and ignorance are now forcibly driving them into that position which they have so long hesitated to assume. *They must establish an independent nationality. . . .*"

The voices of alarm rose. There was not so much a Jewish problem: there was an Emma Lazarus problem!

The Reverend Sabato Morais, a leader of Conservative Judaism in Philadelphia, assailed her "strong advocacy of a Jewish commonwealth to be early planted in Palestine." Didn't Miss Lazarus realize that the time for the fulfilment of the Biblical prophecy had not yet arrived? Didn't she understand that the Jews were too disunited and the Gentiles too hostile? Furthermore, her concept of God was far too kindly. Miss

Lazarus had best worship the stern God of Sinai, else she would be judged and condemned as a false Messiah!

Dr. Abram Isaacs, editor of the weekly, the *Jewish Messenger*, called Emma "A Problematic Champion." He approved the "bold and courageous manner in which she champions the Jews," but alas for the second part of her article in the *Century*, "wherein Miss Lazarus appears as an advocate of the establishment of a Jewish nationality." He was firmly opposed to colonization in Palestine, as he was convinced any right-thinking person must be.

Emma's reactions must have infuriated her critics. She told Philip Cowen: "I saw Dr. Isaac's 'leader' yesterday about myself as a 'Problematic Champion.' I do not know whether you intend to make any reply to him—but if my wishes are to be consulted in the matter, I should greatly prefer to have him treated with silent contempt. Besides, there is nothing in his remarks of sufficient significance or force to call for a reply."

As for the attack of the Philadelphia Reverend: "In referring to me the question of reprinting Mr. Morais' article, it is to me a matter of perfect indifference—and you may follow your own inclinations." Cowen did—and printed Morais' article.

She went serenely on her way with her own writing. Her ideas were clear about a national homeland; she was not suggesting that any American Jews leave the United States. ". . . the most ardent supporter of the scheme does not urge the advisability of an emigration en masse of the whole Jewish people to any particular spot. There is not the slightest necessity for an American Jew, the free citizen of a republic, to rest his hopes upon the foundation of any other nationality soever, or to decide whether he individually would or would not be in favor of residing in Palestine. . . .

". . . The fact that the Jews of America are civilly and religiously emancipated, should be, I take it, our strongest impelling motive for working towards the emancipation of our oppressed brethren. No other Jews in the world can bring to bear upon the enterprise such absolute disinterestedness of aim, such long and intimate familiarity with the blessings and delights of liberty. We must help our less fortunate brethren, not with the condescending patronage of the prosperous, who in self-defense undertake to conceal the social sores of the community by providing a remote hiding place for the outcast and the beggar, but with the keen, human sympathy of men and women who endeavor to defend men and women against outrage and oppression. . . ."

If Emma was not upset, her friends were. Why didn't she try tempering some of her remarks a little, go a little slower? Don't antagonize people, especially not your fellow Jews: to whom inconspicuousness is security . . .

Her barbs pricked so sharp that they stung even in such high places as the front office of the weekly wherein the installments appeared! Cyrus Sulzberger had many imposing titles. He was Superintendent of the Religious School of the Congregation Adereth El. He possessed wealth and influential connections through his interests in a major importing firm. And—he was one of the editors of the *American Hebrew*.

He was incensed as he read over Emma's ringing sentences: "The question is, where are we to look in America for the patriotic Jew whose intellect is sufficiently expanded to accept all the conclusions of science, and yet whose sense of the moral responsibilities and glories bequeathed to him by his ancestors is sufficiently vivid to kindle him into a missionary and a prophet? Is such a one to be found among the orthodox attendants of the Synagogue whose sole idea of Judaism is the preservation of an antiquated body of ceremonials, and in whose ears the very word *Reform* (i.e., Progress, Advance, Improvement) sounds like the death-knell of all they cherish? . . ."

Mr. Sulzberger's anger barely chastened Emma. If he chose to consider himself one of those singled out for attack, that was his business. She relented only a little when she argued the matter with Philip Cowen.

"Perhaps," Cowen suggested, "you would have made your meaning clearer if you had said '*those* orthodox attendants' instead of '*the*.' "

Emma nodded. "Perhaps so. I had not the slightest intention of condemning *all* the orthodox Jews who go to synagogue, as I think was sufficiently proved by my saying later in the article that even there were to be found Jews in whom the need of fire 'was dormant.' I only referred in that objectionable phrase to those orthodox Jews whom I *classified* as clinging to the antiquated ceremonials and repudiating with holy horror the word 'reform.' "

"And you have come in contact with many such?" Cowen asked.

"I have met several," Emma declared, "who consider themselves far better Jews than I, and who think themselves the props and pillars of Judaism, while I, on the contrary, think they are its living disgrace."

"Yes, yes," Cowen went on hurriedly, "but what about Mr. Sulzberger?"

Emma waved her hand in largesse. "If Mr. Sulzberger can be made to see that my remark was *not* a sweeping one, he may modify his views about me."

Yes, she felt, let her critics modify their views about her convictions; she would not, she could not. She had to express her ideas as she felt them. If Mr. Sulzberger was going to take offense at what she said, that was *his* problem. *Her* problem was championing the great mass of her people!

For she had to force the comfortable up from their complacency, as she herself had had to open the windows of her curtained house and look out upon the world. She was not unsympathetic to her friends, she appreciated their solicitude, and she could understand what prompted their attitude that the

Jews were better off well back from the front ranks. . . . It was part of the old, vicious cycle. She wrote about it in one of the weekly installments of her *Epistle:*

". . . As we are at present situated, whatever faculty we acquire only redounds to our ultimate disadvantage, and I know a warm Jewish patriot who grieves whenever he hears of a mark of distinction won by a Jew.

"For as soon as we adopt a new method of earning an honest livelihood, such skill as we happen to develop at it only brings down upon us from our unsuccessful competitors of other races the old charges of monopolizing and of mysterious tribal collusion. . . ."

She went ahead with another *Epistle,* dealing with industrial training. Such training for work, she insisted, was more important for the Jews than the Torah, the Talmud, the Hebrew language, synagogue worship and even circumcision. There must be Jewish schools all over the land to teach some branch of productive industry.

But she could not let the matter rest with mere publication of her ideas. She had to help translate them into action. So she set to work: called upon Dr. Gottheil and other outstanding Jewish figures in New York, gathered them together for discussion—and deeds.

Philip Cowen was in his office, going over the morning's mail. He shook his head ruefully at the familiar envelope before him. He never knew what would be in the next missive from Miss Lazarus!

There were so many—some making small demands on his time, some large; some written almost in a spirit of pique, some infuriating in their casualness; all of them imbued with a sense of life, a gusto for humankind.

Here was one: "I enclose a stanza of poetry for next week's paper—it is from some Spanish Hebrew poet, but I am sorry to say I do not know which one. I have translated this from the original Hebrew, and so am very proud of it as my first effort!"

Here was another: "I have not yet received any copies of last week's *American Hebrew*, and wish you would kindly attend to the matter for me. The *one* I had by mail on Friday is so badly printed as to be almost illegible, and the six promised copies which I always receive and am in the habit of sending to such of my friends as I think may be interested, have not yet appeared. . . ."

Now a mission of charity: "The young man Finkelstein has been to see me this morning—and I have promised to write you a special letter to see if something cannot be done for him in your office. He is in need of forty dollars to eke out his present means of support during the remainder of his university term. According to his testimonials from the Yale faculty, he has acquitted himself so well in his studies that it does seem hard if he is not able to raise this comparatively trifling sum. I can furnish myself ten dollars towards it—five of my own and five from a friend. Do you not know any charitably disposed persons who can contribute towards the remainder?"

And, exasperatingly, on the same subject just a few days later: "I have read your letters in regard to Finklestein, and will ask your messenger to mail them—but I confess I see no reason in the world why *I* should be consulted about his affairs. I have done what I could for him, and think he deserves this present help which he asks—but I must decline following up all the complications of his past history or entering any further into the matter than I have already done . . . and I do not see why the young man should be called upon for his past and his antecedents when there is a question of this kind. But that is no business of mine."

Or she would ask him to do an errand for her: "Will you kindly return for me the accompanying volume of Graetz' *History of the Jews* which I have kept too long, to Mr. Max

Cohen—I do not know his address—but as I got it through
you, I beg you will take charge of its return with my best
thanks and apologies for having kept it so long."

She could be haughty in tone about her own work: "I do
not wish to be hyper-critical or exacting—but I cannot agree
with you that the errors which remain uncorrected in my last
Epistle were '*unimportant*,' though they were very small. In
one instance, I was made guilty of a grammatical blunder, and
in the other the omission of a single word deprived the phrase
of all meaning. As I know you are always anxious and glad to
please me, I should not have written about this matter, if I did
not think it important."

Her letter might be a refusal and a request all in one. "I am
sorry, but I really have not the time to review Mr. Savage's book
of poems—all the more as I cannot find anything very favorable
to say of it—and he has been so courteous to me that I don't
wish to say anything *un*favorable. Do you take the *Jewish
Chronicle* at the office—and if so, would it be asking too much
of you to let me see your copy each week when you have finished
with it? I will return it promptly."

Or her letter could be an out-and-out refusal. "I am very much
obliged to you for your kind offer to be my escort at the meeting
of Dr. Levey's friends—but I shall not avail myself of your
courtesy, as I am already provided with an escort."

(Augustus Levey had resigned as Secretary of the Hebrew
Emigrant Aid Society. He felt they had bitten off more than
they could chew; that their aims were hopelessly idealistic in
trying to assist all. They would be better off if they proposed
shipping back to Europe those refugees who would not be able
to become self-supporting here in America. Emma did not
agree, but she finally consented to hear out all points of view.) So
her note to Cowen went on: "On receipt of a letter from Mr.
Levey stating more clearly the aims and object of the meeting,

I have reconsidered my former decision and hope to be there tomorrow evening."

But Cowen was not to be her escort. Well, at least the final paragraph wound up on a happier key. "The cloth copy of the *Songs of a Semite* is very nice—I was much pleased with its appearance."

He saved all her notes to him; now, this morning, there was another to add to his collection. This time it was an invitation "to a very informal meeting at Dr. Gottheil's house for discussion of the Eastern-Jewish Question. I write with Dr. Gottheil's permission to beg you to be present, as I am especially interested in the subject. We shall not be more than a dozen altogether."

Would he attend? Of course he would! As she knew he would. That meeting initiated a campaign for a technical training-school for Jews. Emma contributed funds and collected money from others. She also suggested that Philip Cowen and another member of the committee be appointed to explore the most outstanding technical schools in the country, so that their project could benefit by past experience. Cowen returned enthusiastically from the trip to report to her what he had seen at the Massachusetts Institute of Technology in Boston, and the Franklin Institute in Philadelphia. Their own plans took shape; the Hebrew Technical Institute was proudly launched.

10

THE PLACE OF AMERICAN JEWS

🌷 While Jewish consciousness had now become the core of her being, Emma continued with her many other interests. Frequently, on Sunday evening, she attended literary "at homes" on the invitation of the Gilders. Richard Watson Gilder, editor of the *Century*, was in a position to bring together the outstanding artistic personalities of the day.

Rose Hawthorne Lathrop, daughter of Nathaniel Hawthorne and herself a writer, who sometimes attended these gatherings with Emma, has recorded her admiration of the ease with which Emma conversed with the celebrities—even with a philosopher like William James. From James, she saw Emma turn to Tommaso Salvini, the Italian actor whose performance as King Lear had all the New York critics swooning, though he spoke not a word in English. But Emma spoke Italian fluently.

Truly, Emma was an extraordinary person. And "of such sweet delicacy of spirit," Rose described her, "never giving the least sign that she did not find a very secure footing for her mental exploration while accompanying a person who knew little Latin and less Greek!"

Not all of Emma's friends were so wholeheartedly approving or admiring. Some challenged her devotion to the Jewish cause. Wasn't she an American citizen, daughter of one of New York's first families? How could she maintain an allegiance to the Jews and to America both? Didn't this make for a dual nationality—for a shifting, alternating standard of values?

On that Emma was adamant. "For ourselves, personally,"

she had declared in her *Epistle*, "we have nothing to ask or desire; neither our national nor our domestic happiness is bound up with the existence of any other Government in the world, than that of the United States."

She felt no conflict; nor should there be in any other Jewish-American mind. Unless, of course, one had a lower estimation of America than she did! A good Jew and a good American had the same ideals: freedom from oppression, liberty of thought ranging as broad and free as the rolling prairies of the West— truth and justice as the goal of a constantly expanding frontier. The "perpetual lamp" was a light to illumine the way. . . .

Instead of the narrow, set ways of the Old World, in these concepts could be found a wide horizon for many nationalities, for all hopeful humanity. Proudly she had claimed: "We possess the double cosmopolitanism of the American and the Jew."

She agreed with Heine that "every country has the Jews it deserves." And, if there were some who did not live up to the noblest standards of humanity, was it not because some countries forced them out of honorable ways of livelihood, and drove them to low and mean practices? For in many places Jews were not only denied the right to own land, and to till the soil, but to engage in any decent occupation. Anti-Semitism forced them to desperate ways to earn their daily bread; anti-Semitism caused them to flee for their very lives.

Emma expressed this degradation caused by anti-Semitism in her vivid dramatic poem, "Raschi in Prague," dealing with the fate of the rabbinical scholar who wrote the first commentary on the Talmud and the Old Testament. Raschi exhorts his Christian captors:

> *"Grace for my tribe! They are what ye have made.*
> *If any be among them fawning, false,*
> *Insatiable, revengeful, ignorant, mean—*
> *And there are many such—ask your own hearts*
> *What virtue ye would yield for planted hate,*
> *Ribald contempt, forced, menial servitude,*

> *Slow centuries of vengeance for a crime*
> *Ye never did commit? Mercy for these!*
> *Who bear on back and breast the scathing brand*
> *Of scarlet degradation, who are clothed*
> *In ignominious livery, whose bowed necks*
> *Are broken with the yoke. Change these to men!*
> *That were a noble witchcraft simply wrought,*
> *God's alchemy transforming clods to gold."*

Yes, Emma felt, every country got the Jews it deserved. And in her own native America, the sweet, democratic country of her birth and all her days she happily exulted that the Jew was a free citizen of a Republic.

American Jews were worthy sons and daughters of a democracy. They would become even more worthy, as America lived up to its ideals. Whenever Emma exposed any home-grown cases of anti-Semitism, it was not out of spite or dislike for her own country, but out of a deep and abiding love. Her America must not shrink in stature, must not reduce itself to petty, bigoted ways. America must rise ever taller in freedom, ever broader in justice.

There was so much to be done, so much for her pen to write! In the few swift months between November and the end of January, she had published fifteen installments of her *Epistle.* A halt had to come sometime! She sent off the sixteenth and last installment to Philip Cowen.

"I trust you will not be too much shocked to find that it is the *Conclusion!"*

In this final installment, she summed up the ideas she had been trying to communicate:

"My chief aim has been to contribute my mite towards arousing that spirit of Jewish enthusiasm which might manifest itself: First, in a return to the varied pursuits and broad system of physical and intellectual education adopted by our ancestors; Second, in a more fraternal and practical movement towards alleviating the sufferings of oppressed Jews in countries less favored than our own; *Third,* in a closer and wider study of Hebrew literature and history; and finally, in a truer recognition of the large principles of religion, liberty, and law upon which Judaism is founded, and which should draw into harmonious unity Jews of every shade of opinion."

She appealed to her readers to put off prejudice and subjectivity: "All that I wish most earnestly to implore from Jews of every variety of political and religious belief, is that they lay aside personal and superficial considerations and approach this subject in the grave spirit which it imperatively demands, and with the cordial desire to ignore all non-essential differences and to meet upon those bases of agreement which must underlie all patriotic Jewish thought, and upon which some substantial project of reform or emancipation may be consentaneously founded.

"The Jew (I say it proudly rather than deprecatingly) is a born rebel. He is endowed with a shrewd, logical mind, in order that he may examine and protest; with a stout and fervent heart, in order that the instinct of liberty may grow into a consuming passion, whereby, if need be, all other impelling motives shall be swallowed up. Such a one reluctantly submits to the restraint of discipline, even if it be imposed by the exigencies of his peculiar lot, in the interests of his own race."

She could not help remembering some of the voices of opposition raised against her, and those who had begun projects with enthusiasm, only to drop out. She was only human; she had to put in one last word on the subject. "To unite in concerted action a people so jealous of their individual privileges, is a task of such difficulty as to be generally deemed impossible. The lesson of discipline and organization is the last one that the Jews will learn; but until they have mastered it, they cannot hope to secure by desultory, independent and often mutually conflicting efforts, equal conditions and human rights for their oppressed brethren."

Portent of spring was in the air when the concluding installment of her *Epistle* appeared. March, with the feeling of a new
wind rising, was on its way.

There had been an earlier vision of spring many years ago
when her mother died, when the first March violet stirred her to
faith and living hope. Again she felt the need of fresh air, of
natural beauty; the need to get away from the dust of libraries.

In early May the family moved from Fifty-seventh Street to
Greenwich Village, to a house at 18 West Tenth Street. There
were trees there, but she needed more than that. A sea-change
would be the most welcome.

To have the tang of ocean spray in her face spicy as pine
needles, to feel the rocking yet restful motion of a ship, to watch
the limitless blue-green horizon spread out before her. . . .

She had made plans to sail to Europe with her friend Rose
Hawthorne Lathrop. But because of the demands of her family,
Rose could not accompany Emma for another year.

Too impatient to wait, Emma took one of her younger sisters
along as a companion and sailed on the S.S. "Alaska," on May
15, 1883.

Philip Cowen smiled as he waved farewell. The ever-paradoxi-
cal Miss Lazarus! She needed a rest, a change of scene, yet she
took her own portable landscape with her. She had asked him
for letters of introduction to representative Jewish figures in
England and France. . . . Surely she was not going to meet with
them merely to discuss the differences in American and European
weather!

And her letter to him of last week acknowledging the gift of
a book in a fine binding, given by a group associated with her
in the Jewish cause. He could recall the words: "I was completely
taken by surprise on my return home late last night," Emma
wrote him, "to find myself the recipient of so much honor and
such a splendid gift. I thank you most sincerely as a member
of the society, as well as for the special trouble which I know

has fallen to you in the selection of my book. I could not have desired anything more beautiful and appropriate."

Then she had gone on, in the same paragraph, to reflect on herself—truly her modesty was amazing: "The work I have done for the Jewish Cause seems to me painfully insignificant and slight, compared with the generous sympathy and encouragement I receive from my people. I can only hope by continuing my efforts, to be some day, worthy of such kind words and deeds."

Cowen hoped fervently that the world would be worthy of her kind words and deeds. She scarcely needed the letters of introduction he and Michael Heilprin and Dr. Gottheil had provided. Her fame had preceded her. The most distinguished Jews of England were waiting to greet her.

11

INTERNATIONAL HORIZONS

❦ The ocean voyage was as restful and as refreshing as Emma hoped. She wrote: "Our last day on board ship was a vision of beauty from morning till night—the sea like a mirror and the sky dazzling with light. . . ."

The seascape was lulling; it was the rest she needed. But the human landscape was infinitely more inviting. "In the afternoon we passed a ship in full sail, near enough to exchange salutes and cheers. . . . After tossing about for six days without seeing a human being, except those on our vessel, even this was a sensation. Then an hour or two before sunset came the great sensation of—land! At first, nothing but a shadow on the far horizon, like the ghost of a ship; two or three widely scattered rocks which were the promontories of Ireland, and sooner than we expected, we were steaming among low-lying purple hills."

Then on to the village of Chester for her "first glimpse of mellow England." The streets were picturesquely winding and narrow, "like the scene of a Walter Scott novel, the cathedral planted in greenness, and the clear, gray river where a boatful of scarlet dragoons goes gliding by."

Everything looked just as it should; she was delighted as the historic countryside unfolded before her. It was the England she had envisioned from her reading, yet each sight was thrillingly new, each hour had for her the impact of a poem. Emma noted: "I drink in, at every sense, the sights, sounds, and smells, and the unimaginable beauty of it all."

In London there were teas, receptions, dinner parties, meetings with outstanding Jews who shared her opinions on a Jewish

restoration in Palestine. Her bold *Epistle* had made her known
abroad.

And Emma was also well-regarded in England as a poet.
English critics had acclaimed her talent from her very first book
of lyrics and translations. Indeed, in some respects, they had
overpraised her—as when some compared her romantic verse
dramas to those of Robert Browning and William Morris to
their disparagement.

But there could be no mistake about *Songs of a Semite*. This
was the performance of an important poet at the height of her
power.

Edmund Gosse, the critic, the poet Austin Dobson, Georgiana
and Edward Burne-Jones, the artist, Thomas Huxley, the
scientist, and his wife, Henrietta, Henry James, and other nota-
bles sought her out.

For all Emma's shyness in public, she was completely at ease
at informal gatherings. Her sister Josephine, who became an
author herself on Jewish themes, and of biographies of emancipated women, among them Madame Dreyfus, the artist Marie
Bashkirtseff, and the feminist, Margaret Fuller, thus described
Emma at this period: "There was, no doubt, something that
strongly attracted and attached people to her at this time—the
force of her intellect at once made itself felt, while at the same
time the unaltered simplicity and modesty of her character, and
her readiness and freshness of enthusiasm, kept her still almost
like a child."

Her appearance expressed the contradictions in her personality.
Dark-eyed, serious-browed, she struck some as over-serious. "Her
face was a forest densely populated with thoughts." To another,
she was "the most feminine of women." To a third, her face
reflected changing moods. At first she might seem "mutinous
and inclined to be sarcastic, yet in a moment, her brow cleared,
her eye lightened, she became gentle and tender."

That June was a month of flowering. She mingled with

poets and politicians, lords and ladies. Maude Stanley, daughter of the Lord of Alderley, no typical child of the idle rich but a writer on social problems, and a friend of Thomas Carlyle, sought to exchange ideas with Emma. Maude Stanley had recently opened a recreation center—the first club for working girls.

But the high point for Emma was her meeting with Robert Browning, whom she admired enormously as a poet, and as a man of principled conviction. Roused to anger by the pogroms in Russia, he had petitioned for English intervention. Like herself, he had become an enthusiastic student of the Hebrew language. He had many Jewish friends, some dating back to the period when his father had clerked for the famous banker, Rothschild.

Browning's fame was international. There were nearly as many Browning Societies in America as in England. Browning invited Emma to visit in the house he now shared with his sister Sarrina after the death of his beloved wife, Elizabeth Barrett. If that was not convenient, he would be glad to call at Miss Lazarus' hotel. The mountain bowing to Mahomet!

Emma was thrilled to visit the Browning house. The poet was now a white-haired man in his seventies. The memory of her first visit to Emerson's home in Concord must have flashed through her mind as she crossed the threshold.

Though full of reverence toward Browning, Emma had never been one to sit in silent worship. She had questions to put to him. Philip Cowen had asked that if she met Browning, she must get him to clear up certain obscurities in some of his lines. Browning smiled. The lines she was inquiring about had been written several generations ago—how could he possibly recollect what was in that young Browning's head? He had questions for her: How could a certain Hebrew passage be most accurately translated into English? The two heads, one white with age, the other darkly bright, bent over the book. Later, he took her

through the house, showed her souvenirs of his poet wife—
her shawl, her jewels, her photographs, manuscripts. The visit
was all too short for both of them. Browning asked her to visit
again.

She promised, but she had not yet been to the Continent!
With her younger sister, she crossed over to France, arriving in
Paris on July 14th—Bastille Day, anniversary of the Republic.

No freedom was ever gained without sacrifice, she observed, as
they were guided through the streets. She wrote: "There are
ruins on every side—ruins of the Commune, or the Siege, or the
Revolution; it is terrible—it seems as if the city were seared
with fire and blood." Driving out in a carriage from Paris to
Versailles, it seemed to her "a gorgeous shell of royalty, where
the crowd who celebrate the birth of the republic wander freely
through the halls and avenues. . . ."

She returned to England, with its calmer countryside, where
the extremes seemed less violent. A day she had been eagerly
anticipating was at last before her—she was on her way to
Surrey to meet William Morris.

Morris was a many-sided man; an outstanding poet and
handicraft designer, and, as a follower of Marx, one of the
founders of the Democratic Federation, the first Socialist organization in England. Morris spoke in meeting rooms, and on
street-corners when a hall could not be hired. He sold his private
library to raise funds for the cause, edited a Socialist newspaper,
wrote *Chants for Socialists*. His rank as a poet was high enough
for him to be considered for the post of Poet Laureate when
Tennyson died, but he refused because it might call for compro-
mising his political convictions.

His dream was a just society, not an idle one. There would
be work for all, but the work would be satisfying to all. No
man should exploit his brother—or sister. Morris envisioned
women of the future freed from Victorian hypocrisy and restrictions. Thus they would become more, not less womanly.

In an attempt to put some of his social and political theories into action, he had set up a co-operative factory where the workers shared in the profits. Today, he was to show Emma through it. It was located in an abandoned Norman monastery, Merton Abbey in Surrey. Its landscaped acres breathed history. "Yes," said Morris, "this place hangs doubtful between the past and the present." But he was not the least doubtful about the future. A man's labor should not be exploited by another; he himself should share in the fruits of his labor. "No man," he argued, "is good enough to be any other's master." So the profit-sharing workshop at the Abbey had been blueprinted as Morris' glimpse of the future. There the craftsmen sold and profited from the chairs, rugs, wall coverings, they made with their own hands. In Morris' opinion, mass production was ruining the essential beauty and worth of things.

He showed Emma the materials they worked with at the Abbey. "You see?" he held up a hand-woven swatch of fabric. "I have tried to produce goods which should be genuine as far as their mere substances are concerned, and should have on that account the primary beauty in them which belongs to naturally treated substances. I have tried for instance to make woolen substances as woolen as possible, cotton as cottony as possible."

"And the dyestuffs?" Emma asked.

"Only those which are natural and simple—because they produce beauty almost without the intervention of art."

It was his aim that the masses who had to be content with inferior goods, should some day enjoy well-crafted objects. Yes, life with all its utensils should be beautified for the many. There should not be luxuries for a few, just as poetry should not be merely for a rarefied circle. He repeated his credo: "I do not want art for a few, any more than education for a few or freedom for a few."

Emma's tour of the British Isles continued through the sum-

mer. Morris' passionately expressed philosophy came back to her
again and again as she saw flower-laden gardens, softly rolling
hills. Yes, how fine it would be if some day all could enjoy this
beauty. In Kent, she noted, "the fields, valleys and slopes are
garlanded with hops and ablaze with scarlet poppies." She saw
the cathedral of Canterbury, the bell towers of Oxford, the
Shakespeare country around Stratford, took the train north as far
as Edinburgh in Scotland. Her spirits soared, on "a crescendo of
enjoyment."

But September was here already—how quickly her four
months had gone by!—and it was time to return home. For in
autumn, in the abundant harvest season, how could she be
anywhere except in her native America?

Emma Lazarus Memorial Plaque, Battery Park, Manhattan, 1973.
(This foundation stone was the gift of the State of Israel; presented
by the Federation of Jewish Women's Organizations.)
NYC Parks Photo Archive

East 14th St. brownstone houses bordering 5th Ave., NY in the 1850's.
At 36 West 14th St., Emma Lazarus lived in similar surroundings.

Castle Garden at the Battery, NY, about 1850. Immigrants entering before 1892
were processed there. (Later arrivals entered at Ellis Island in NY Harbor)

Union Square around 1854. (See Chapter 1)

The Lazarus family summer home, "The Beeches" at 647 Bellevue Ave.,
Newport, R.I..

Redwood Library and Athenaeum Newport, R.I.
Photo reproduction of plate by John Corbett

The last known address of Emma Lazarus in NYC at
18 West 10th St., and where she died on Nov. 19, 1887.

photo by B.G. Gold

Emma Lazarus' grave in Shearith Israel IV (Beth Olom) section of the Cypress Hills cemetery, Brooklyn, NY.
Photo by C.H. Halporn of rubbing of bronze plaque by Roberta Halporn

12

THE TORCH HELD HIGH

🌺 Emma returned to New York with rejuvenated strength. Again she became a busy committee member, raising funds for the refugees, and writing articles and poems for such occasions as the eight-day holiday of Chanukah.

THE FEAST OF LIGHTS

Kindle the taper like the steadfast star
Ablaze on evening's forehead o'er the earth,
And add each night a lustre till afar
An eightfold splendor shine above thy hearth.
Clash, Israel, the cymbals, touch the lyre,
Blow the brass trumpet and the harsh-tongued horn;
Chant psalms of victory till the heart take fire,
The Maccabean spirit leap new-born.

Remember how from wintry dawn till night,
Such songs were sung in Zion, when again
On the high altar flamed the sacred light,
And, purified from every Syrian stain,
The foam-white walls with golden shields were hung,
With crowns and silken spoils, and at the shrine,
Stood, midst their conqueror-tribe, five chieftains sprung
From one heroic stock, one seed divine.

As the base of the *menorah* is a strong root like a tree, with branches curving upward to hold a candle for each Chanukah day, so her poem visualizes the Maccabean clan—the five hero-warriors sprung from the parental tree:

Five branches grow from Mattathias' stem,
The Blessed John, the Keen-Eyed Jonathan,
Simon, the fair, the Burst-of-Spring, the Gem,
Eleazer, Help-of-God; o'er all his clan
Judas the Lion-Prince, the Avenging Rod,
Towered in warrior-beauty, uncrowned king,

Armed with the breastplate and the sword of God,
Whose praise is: "He received the perishing!"

They who had camped within the mountain-pass,
Couched on the rock, and tented neath the sky,
Who saw from Mizpah's heights the tangled grass
Choke the wide Temple-courts, the altar lie
Disfigured and polluted—who had flung
Their faces on the stones, and mourned aloud
And rent their garments, wailing with one tongue,
Crushed as a wind-swept bed of reeds is bowed.

Even they by one voice fired, one heart of flame,
Though broken reeds, had risen, and were men,
They rushed upon the spoiler and o'ercame;
Each arm for freedom had the strength of ten.
Now is their mourning into dancing turned,
Their sackcloth doffed for garments of delight,
Week-long the festive torches shall be burned,
Music and revelry wed day with night.

Still ours the dance, the feast, the glorious Psalm,
The mystic lights of emblem, and the Word.
Where is our Judas? Where our five-branched palm?
Where are the lion-warriors of the Lord?
Clash, Israel, the cymbals, touch the lyre,
Sound the brass trumpet and the harsh-tongued horn,
Chant hymns of victory till the heart take fire,
The Maccabean spirit leap new-born!

Her Chanukah poem was more than a religious poem; it was a call to the spirit and to action. As the Maccabean clan, saddened by the destruction of the Temple of Jerusalem, had risen out of sorrow to strength, to battle for their people, so today, Emma pleaded, let that "spirit leap new-born."

Once, Emma had protested to Dr. Gottheil that she could not compose hymns, because she lacked the requisite religious fervor; and to Philip Cowen that she was unable to write a poem on the Jewish New Year, "on order." Now she was ordering herself, out of her own ardor for her people, out of the needs of the urgent times.

Yet she continued to claim that she could not write on assignment. This time to her old friend, William Evarts, who had spoken at the first protest meeting in Manhattan against the Russian pogroms. Well she remembered his words: "It is the oppression of men and women by men and women that we are concerned with—and we are men and women!"

Evarts was calling on her in behalf of a committee to raise funds for a pedestal for the huge statue to be erected on Bedloe's Island in New York harbor.

A gift from the people of France to the United States, the French sculptor Auguste Bartholdi had executed the statue on a truly immense scale. A mighty base would be required for it.

Emma liked the name of the statue: "Liberty Enlightening the World." She also liked Bartholdi's conception: the figure of Liberty was a woman, with a torch upheld to the sky, like hope reaching across the ocean.

Abstracted with her own images, she scarcely listened to Evarts.

"The committee has been using various methods to raise money for the pedestal," he was saying. "One plan is to hold a literary auction." He mentioned among the writers whose manuscripts were to be offered, Longfellow, Whitman, Mark Twain, Bret Harte. They would like to include the manuscript of a new poem by her. Emma was familiar with the gallery at the corner of Fourth Avenue and Twenty-third Street, was she not?

Emma nodded absently.

"Well, then, it's agreed."

"No!" Emma said. She could not possibly write to order. But after Evarts left, she went to her writing desk.

The statue was colossal, yet not the least like the ancient Colossus of Rhodes, arrogantly bestriding the harbor entrance. This was Liberty, the universal mother, bringing home the wandering children of Israel—the exiles everywhere.

The sonnet came to her quickly; it was to endure forever.

THE NEW COLOSSUS

Not like the brazen giant of Greek fame,
With conquering limbs astride from land to land;
Here at our sea-washed, sunset gates shall stand
A mighty woman with a torch, whose flame
Is the imprisoned lightning, and her name
Mother of Exiles. From her beacon-hand
Glows world-wide welcome; her mild eyes command
The air-bridged harbor that twin cities frame.
"Keep, ancient lands, your storied pomp!" cries she
With silent lips. "Give me your tired, your poor,
Your huddled masses yearning to breathe free,
The wretched refuse of your teeming shore.
Send these, the homeless, tempest-tost to me,
I lift my lamp beside the golden door!"

She marked the date—1883—at the bottom of the page and, as though it might be an ephemeral poem to be forgotten unless annotated, added in parentheses "Written in aid of Bartholdi's Pedestal Fund."

The sonnet was immediately hailed.

The poet James Russell Lowell, then American Ambassador to England wrote to her from London: "I liked your sonnet about the Statue much better than I like the Statue itself. But your sonnet gives its subject a *raison d'être* which it wanted before quite as much as it wanted a pedestal. You have set it on a noble one, saying admirably just the right word to be said, an achievement more arduous than that of the sculptor."

That winter in New York was cold, the wind biting and bitter. Emma thought longingly of the past summer in England and of William Morris whom she had met there. She wrote to him: might she do an article about his model factory, for the American magazine, the *Century?*

Morris wrote back enthusiastically. "Thanks for your kind letter: I should be very pleased that you should write the account you propose: and perhaps if I saw the Ms. I might set straight any matter of fact that had gone awry: of course I would touch nothing else.

"The 'cause' is progressing here: we have now a flourishing branch of the Democratic Federation at Merton Abbey; so you see, I live in hopes of being able to cast my capitalist skin and become a harmless proletarian."

Emma began making notes for her article on Morris, but the writing went slowly. She put it aside in favor of her first love—poetry. She felt compelled to sum up some of her beliefs about the "Jewish Idea." But what kind of poem could it be? She would not be able to contain her ideas in the smallness of a sonnet, or the measured melody of a lyric. Even blank verse, with its regular five-beat line, would be restricting.

So she conceived of a new kind of poetry for herself, freed from the restraints of conventional form. Walt Whitman had spread his message of humanity in sprawling, oceanic sentences. Emma was not Whitman; she was neither that enormous nor that careless. Yet the unconfined form of the prose-poem was what she now needed.

Her pen raced across the pages. In urgent, hard-packed sentences, "By The Waters of Babylon" took shape.

It was more like a motion picture than a poem. Successive scenes filled with a host of figures—with now one, now another emerging into close-ups. The history of the Jews marched past, from the darkness of ages gone, into the burning light of the present.

Little Poems in Prose, as she modestly referred to it, was destined to be her final published work. Several years later, when it appeared in the March, 1887, issue of the *Century,* critics declared that her words "glowed with a gleam of the solemn fire of the Hebrew prophets."

The first passage bears the title "The Exodus" and the date "August 3, 1492." This was the "two-faced year" that she had summoned up before, when the Jews were expelled from Spain and when Columbus set forth on his voyage to the New World. Now her language is more impassioned; it is a cry of fearful lamentation and of exultant strength.

1. *The Spanish noon is a blaze of azure fire, and the dusty pilgrims crawl like an endless serpent along treeless plains and bleached high-roads, through rock-split ravines and castellated, cathedral-shadowed towns.*

2. *The hoary patriarch, wrinkled as an almond shell, bows painfully upon his staff. The beautiful young mother, ivory-pale, well-nigh swoons beneath her burden; in her large enfolding arms nestles her sleeping babe, round her knees flock her little ones with bruised and bleeding feet. "Mother, shall we soon be there?"*

3. *The youth with Christ-like countenance speaks comfortably to father and brother, to maiden and wife. In his breast, his own heart is broken.*

4. *The halt, the blind, are amid the train. Sturdy pack-horses laboriously drag the tented wagons wherein lie the sick athirst with fever.*

5. *The panting mules are urged forward with spur and goad; stuffed are the heavy saddle-bags with the wreckage of ruined homes.*

6. *Hark to the tinkling silver bells that adorn the tenderly-carried silken scrolls.*

7. *In the fierce noon-glare a lad bears a kindled lamp; behind its network of bronze the airs of heaven breathe not upon its faint purple star.*

8. *Noble and abject, learned and simple, illustrious and obscure, plod side by side, all brothers now, all merged in one routed army of misfortune.*

9. *Woe to the straggler who falls by the wayside! No friend shall close his eyes.*

10. *They leave behind the grape, the olive, and the fig; the vines they planted, the corn they sowed, the garden-cities of Andalusia and Aragon, Estremadura and La Mancha, of Granada and Castile; the altar, the hearth, and the grave of their fathers.*

11. *The townsman spits at their garments, the shepherd quits his flock, the peasant his plow, to pelt with curses and stones; the villager sets on their trail his yelping cur.*

12. *Oh the weary march, oh the uptorn roots of home, oh the blankness of the receding goal!*

13. *Listen to their lamentation:* They that ate dainty food are desolate in the streets; they that were reared in scarlet embrace dunghills. They flee away and wander about. Men say among the nations, they shall no more sojourn there; our end is near, our days are full, our doom is come.

14. *Whither shall they turn? for the West hath cast them out, and the East refuseth to receive.*

15. *O bird of the air, whisper to the despairing exiles, that today, today, from the many-masted, gayly-bannered port of Palos, sails the world-unveiling Genoese, to unlock the golden gates of sunset and bequeath a Continent to Freedom!*

In the section entitled "Currents," she writes of the modern Jews fleeing the pogroms of Russia, finding refuge in America:

1. *Vast oceanic movements, the flux and reflux of immeasurable tides oversweep our continent.*

2. *From the far Caucasian steppes, from the squalid Ghettos of Europe,*

3. *From Odessa and Bucharest, from Kief and Ekaterinoslav,*

4. *Hark to the cry of the exiles of Babylon, the voice of Rachel mourning for her children, of Israel lamenting for Zion.*

5. *And lo, like a turbid stream, the long-pent flood bursts the dykes of oppression and rushes hitherward.*

6. *Unto her ample breast, the generous mother of nations welcomes them.*

7. *The herdsman of Canaan and the seed of Jerusalem's royal shepherd renew their youth amid the pastoral plains of Texas and the golden valleys of the Sierras.*

Some time later, a critic discussing American patriotic poems, commented on this passage: "Have you seen a prose poem called 'Currents' which celebrates this as the mother-country of all lands? Of course it is so broadly national that there is no war in it."

In the sixth section, "The Prophet," Emma returns to the image she has ever held high: the "perpetual lamp"—her lamp of truth, of justice, the torch she has uplifted herself. She summons the great scholars and singers before her, before us all:

1. *Moses Ben Maimon lifting his perpetual lamp over the path of the perplexed;*

2. *Halevi, the honey-tongued poet, wakening amid the silent ruins of Zion the sleeping lyre of David;*

3. *Moses, the wise son of Mendel, who made the Ghetto illustrious;*

4. *Abarbanel, the counselor of kings; Alcharisi, the exquisite singer; Ibn Ezra, the perfect old man; Gabirol, the tragic seer;*

5. *Heine, the enchanted magician, the heart-broken jester;*

6. *Yea, and the century-crowned patriarch whose bounty encircles the globe;—*

7. *These need no wreath and no trumpet; like perennial asphodel blossoms, their fame, their glory resounds like the brazen-throated cornet.*

8. *But thou—hast thou faith in the fortune of Israel? Wouldst thou lighten the anguish of Jacob?*

9. *Then shalt thou take the hand of yonder caftaned wretch with flowing curls and gold-pierced ears;*

10. *Who crawls blinking forth from the loathsome recesses of the Jewry;*

11. *Nerveless his fingers, puny his frame; haunted by the batlike phantoms of superstition is his brain.*

12. *Thou shalt say to the bigot, "My Brother," and to the creature of darkness, "My Friend."*

13. *And thy heart shall spend itself in fountains of love upon the ignorant, the coarse, and the abject.*

14. *Then in the obscurity thou shalt hear a rush of wings, thine eyes shall be bitten with pungent smoke.*

15. *And close against thy quivering lips shall be pressed the live coal wherewith the Seraphim brand the Prophets.*

After completing "By the Waters of Babylon," she returned to work on the Morris article. It proceeded, but still slowly, and again she interrupted the writing for further poems.

William Morris had made his choice as to the kind of society he wished to live in. He had set up a high standard of moral values for himself, and had the courage to abide by his faith. Emma was no less proud of the faith of the Jewish people. She contrasted the different paths offered to conscience in her poem "The Choice":

> *I saw in dream the spirits unbegot,*
> *Veiled, floating phantoms, lost in twilight space;*
> *For one the hour had struck, he paused; the place*
> *Rang with an awful Voice:*
>   *"Soul, choose thy lot!*
> *Two paths are offered; that, in velvet-flower,*
> *Slopes easily to every earthly prize.*
> *Follow the multitude and bind thine eyes,*
> *Thou and thy sons' sons shall have peace with power.*
> *This narrow track skirts the abysmal verge,*
> *Here shalt thou stumble, totter, weep and bleed,*

All men shall hate and hound thee and thy seed,
Thy portion be the wound, the stripe, the scourge.
But in thy hand I place my lamp for light,
Thy blood shall be the witness of my Law,
Choose now for all the ages!"
                    Then I saw
The unveiled spirit, grown divinely bright,
Choose the grim path. He turned, I knew full well
The pale, great martyr-forehead shadowy-curled,
The glowing eyes that had renounced the world,
Disgraced, despised, immortal Israel.

The *American Hebrew* printed "The Choice" in April, 1884; it was widely praised and read aloud at public gatherings.

But there were times when Emma felt it was discreet not to have her name so often in the pages of Cowen's weekly. She had become so known as a writer on Jewish affairs, she thought her ideas might sometimes have more weight if they were not attributed to her. For if you constantly cry out—even though there is good cause to exclaim!—people sooner or later might disregard the cry because the voice had become too familiar. "Oh yes, Emma Lazarus again, harping on the same old theme. . . ."

She had been struck by an item in the *Boston Journal.* That newspaper was virtuously condemning London hotel-owners who were reported to be refusing to house American tourists who happened to be Jews. It seemed most ironic to Emma that while the Boston paper moralized against the English it uttered no word against the American hotels that practiced the same restrictions!

Titling her piece, "A Bit of British Impudence," she sent it off to Cowen with a warning note. "I should like to have you print the accompanying in this week's *American Hebrew* WITHOUT MY SIGNATURE. Can you make room for it as an editorial? I particularly wish that it should appear anonymously, as my name cannot help it."

Emma had become so immersed in the "Jewish Idea," as she termed it, that she had been almost oblivious of her protesting body. She was impatient that the need for rest came so frequently. Too many precious hours had to be given over to sleep —how much more she could accomplish, how much more she could study and enrich her mind, if only that nagging partner, her body, did not insist upon attention! But insist it did, and she had to stop writing and studying, and to halt, relax.

Her most rewarding hours of relaxation came when she listened to the music of her two beloved composers, Bach and Beethoven. Yet they stimulated her as well. She could not altogether keep her mind from functioning; her happiest leisure hours served to spur her on.

The *American Hebrew* announced an essay contest under the auspices of the Young Men's Hebrew Association. Manuscripts on Jewish themes were to be submitted anonymously. Emma could not resist this challenge.

Her subject was "M. Renan and the Jews," and she signed it "Esther Sarazal."

Her essay won the prize, was read aloud at a "monthly entertainment" of the Y.M.H.A., and later published in the *American Hebrew*.

The ideas of the French scholar, Ernest Renan, had seemed to Emma worth exploring for a Jewish audience. An authority on Hebrew and other Eastern languages, Renan had written *The Life of Jesus* and *History of the People of Israel*. Many of his colleagues considered his opinions far too liberal. What a pity, some thought privately, that he was so eminent in his field he could not be dislodged from his post at the Collège de France!

Renan, the Christian scholar, shared Emma's conviction that "in the prophetic books are laid down, on broad bases, the foundations of a universal religion. A religion that preaches the purest spiritual monotheism, the abolition of sacrifices and ritualism, the necessity of the moral law, the brotherhood of man, and the ultimate reign of peace and justice."

"Christianity," he proclaimed, "is Judaism adapted to Indo-

European taste, Mahometanism is Judaism adapted to Arabic taste. . . . The pure religion which we foresee, that will prove capable of rallying all humanity to its standard, will be the realization of the religion of Isaiah, *the ideal Jewish religion,* purged of the dross that may have been mixed with it. . . . Let us say it boldly, Judaism which has done such service in the past will serve also in the future. It will serve the true cause, the cause of liberalism and of the modern spirit."

Renan's sentences, to Emma, were like the triumphal blast of the *shofar* bringing down walls of prejudice and separation. In her essay she wrote: "Such words as these send a thrill of exultation through the veins of every true Jew; not the unworthy pride of a flattered egotism, but the glorious sense of an inconceivably noble vocation. Nothing less than the universal welfare, bought at this price, could compensate the Hebrew race for having served through history as the type of suffering. Not for the mere survival of this little band of martyrs and victims was the miracle of their endurance prolonged; but because the seed of truth, which they alone cherished through fire and blood, had not yet borne its highest, sweetest and ripest fruit."

The seed of truth, and the fruit thereof. Not in the narrow plot of an unattainable Garden of Eden, but in the wide workaday world, in the cause of her people, of all peoples of the earth.

13

THE BATTLE FOR CONSCIENCE

🌷 Demands on her time, her talents, continued to pour in. She gave of both willingly. But to the third demand—public appearance before an audience—her answer continued to be "No." So she wrote to Dr. Solomon Solis-Cohen who had asked her to address the Philadelphia Y.M.H.A.: ". . . anything in the nature of a lecture or an address is entirely beyond my province and capacity—and I must decline with thanks your invitation."

In a softer tone her letter continued: "I may add, however, that my interest in the culture and improvement of American Jews, makes me anxious to serve their cause to the poor extent of my ability—and if I could be of any service to you by contributing an Essay which one of your staff, or Society might read for me in my absence, I shall be glad to do so.

"If this plan meets with your approval, I should prefer to have you suggest such themes as you deem suitable and necessary for your audience. I can generally write best when I know clearly what is wanted from me."

A few months later, she was writing to Dr. Solis-Cohen again: "I have written the Essay which I promised you. After considering all your kindly-suggested topics, I suddenly had an impulse to select my own theme, which is the Bar-Kochba Rebellion. If you care so far in advance to read the paper, it is at your disposal. I hope it will not prove too historical or too 'dry' for the purpose you design."

Philip Cowen had lent her the volume of Graetz's *History of the Jews* in which she had read of the heroic Bar-Kochba.

The revolt he led in Judea in the year 135, against the Roman occupation, seemed to Emma to have heightened significance now, for Americans, and for Jewish-Americans especially. She saw in Bar-Kochba's rebellion the very principles upon which the United States was founded.

"In that little Judaic tribe," she wrote, "I see the spiritual fathers of those who braved exile and death for conscience's sake, to found upon the New England rocks, within the Pennsylvania woods, over this immense continent, the Republic of the West. I see in Bar-Kochba, the ignored, despised, defeated Jewish soldier, the same passion of patriotism which under more fortunate conditions, made illustrious a William of Orange (the English monarch whose reign produced the Constitution of 1689), a Mazzini, a Garibaldi (nineteenth century heroes of the Italian democratic revolution), a Kossuth (leader of the 1848 revolution in Hungary), a Washington. . . ."

The ideals Bar-Kochba had fought for, were "the Jewish Idea—the idea of protest, of revolution against moral tyranny, of inviolable freedom of thought and conscience."

Emma brought Bar-Kochba's revolt blazingly alive. "When Hadrian ascended the imperial throne . . . the active or sullen resistance of the Jewish people against the Roman yoke had already lasted nearly two centuries. . . . This monarch . . . resolved to annihilate Judean nationality and blot out the very name of Jerusalem. . . . From Egypt his commands were issued that the plough be passed over the ruined site of the Temple, that the rite of circumcision be abolished, and that Jerusalem be rebuilt as a Pagan city. . . . These three fatal measures were the signal for revolt: the Sanhedrin was convoked with Akiba at its head, and a war for death or victory was unanimously resolved upon.

"The rebellion seemed to break out over night; while, during Hadrian's visit, all Palestine had appeared tranquilly submissive, on the morrow of his departure two hundred thousand Jews

sprang to arms. The movement, however, was less sudden than
it appeared, otherwise it would have lacked the organized force
and solidity which it actually evinced in the three years'
struggle. . . .

"The Jewish artisans who were in the habit of supplying
arms to the Roman soldiers, were found to have deliberately
manufactured weak and worthless weapons. Judea was honey-
combed with subterranean caves underneath its chalky hills, and
in these the conspirators had met and not only perfected their
deep and cautious plans, but had deposited their own skillfully
wrought weapons of defense. The venerable Rabbi Akiba, the
head of the community, had taken secret but active steps toward
strengthening, extending and consolidating the general movement. He had traveled far and wide, instigating to revolt the
Jews of Parthia, Asia Minor, Cappodicia, Phrygia and Galatia.
When, therefore, the insurrection broke out, everything was in
readiness—arms, methods of communication, soldiers and even
a leader.

"This leader was Bar-Kochba, 'The Son of a Star,' who seems
to embody in one last supreme manifestation the martial spirit
of his people. . . . The Jews of all the neighboring lands flocked
to his standard; even their immemorial adversaries, the Samar-
itans, enrolled in his ranks, which were further swelled by troops
of disaffected Pagans who made common cause with the Israelites
in hope of shaking off the intolerable dominion of Rome. . . .

"Inch by inch, the Latins regained the territory that Bar-
Kochba had recovered from them in his brief campaign. Fifty-
two distinct engagements had occurred, when the circle of
Jewish possessions, gradually narrowing, had reduced itself to
a single spot, and the whole Jewish army was besieged in the
town of Bethar. Within the walls, the Son of a Star, the last
King of the Jews, directed and organized the defense, and pun-
ished with death whoever spoke of yielding, while the aged
Akiba stimulated the beleaguered army with the example of

his fortitude and patriotism, and presided over the Council of Ten who aided and advised the military leaders. . . .

"The siege lasted a year; when it became evident that the end was approaching, a very old man, Rabbi Eleazer Hamodai, proclaimed that the only hope left was in prayer, and day and night he fasted and watched upon his knees in a conspicuous position, praying for Bar-Kochba's success. . . .

"A general massacre of the inhabitants followed the entrance of the Roman troops, whose horses waded to the neck in blood. . . . Akiba and the nine rabbis who with him had formed the council of defense were condemned to death by torture. . . . Akiba was the last to suffer, being compelled to witness the agonies of all his companions. He was burned at the stake, and his flesh torn with iron instruments. . . .

"A dismembered nation, a territory laid waste and usurped by the stranger, a prohibited region, a Temple blotted from the earth, a capital wiped out of existence in name and fact, and a decimated tribe of exiles and slaves—such were the immediate results of the last fatal revolt of the Jews in 135. . . .

"But no! through all history was to run the dark, rich stream of Jewish life and thought, sometimes dwindling into a mere pulsing thread, sometimes broadening into a powerful current, intersecting or flowing parallel with all the great historic streams, never losing its peculiar force and virtue. . . .''

In a short poem bearing the hero's name, Emma summed up the indomitable spirit of Bar-Kochba:

> Weep, Israel! your tardy meed outpour
>   Of grateful homage on his fallen head,
> That never coronal of triumph wore,
>   Untombed, dishonored, and unchapleted.
> If Victory makes the hero, raw Success
>   The stamp of virtue, unremembered
> Be then the desperate strife, the storm and stress
>   Of the last Warrior Jew. But if the man
> Who dies for freedom, loving all things less,
>   Against world-legions, mustering his poor clan;

> *The weak, the wronged, the miserable, to send*
> *Their death-cry's protest through the ages' span—*
> *If such an one be worthy, ye shall lend*
> *Eternal thanks to him, eternal praise.*
> *Nobler the conquered than the conqueror's end!*

Inspired though she was, nevertheless she felt a weight pressing her down. On the clearest blue-sky day, the air seemed swollen, distended, as if she had to push her way through fog. Was it just the sultry heat of this August of 1884?

Others did not seem to mind it; there had been more uncomfortable New York summers. But for Emma, walking, which used to be such a free-striding pleasure, now became a tiring effort. Her head ached.

Something was wrong. Her family and her friends urged her to see a doctor. But even specialists could not determine the cause.

Then, almost miraculously, her sickness disappeared as it had come, without warning. By autumn, her beloved season, she felt quite well again. The doctors shrugged. Accept health as a gift and do not question it. But they warned Emma that she must conserve her energies in the future. The weakness could return—and it did.

At the end of October, she wrote to Philip Cowen: "I am sorry there has been delay in returning my proofs to you—but I was not able even to look at them till this morning—as I have not yet my full strength, and was too tired when I came home late yesterday, to do so much as to open them. . . . I return herewith the volume of George Eliot—as I am not well enough to undertake any literary work for the present, and cannot give my mind to this. I have no doubt you will find a suitable reviewer—I thank you for your kind inquiries about my health. I have entirely recovered from my illness, but shall have to be cautious about overtaxing my strength for some time to come."

Then, as Emma was recuperating, her father took sick. Her

heart ached to see him in pain. As autumn drew into winter, his pain became constant. The cheerful home became a house of shadows. What were the chances for recovery? Was there any hope for a partial improvement, for at least an easing of pain? The harsh fact had to be faced, said the doctors, that he could look forward to a few more months of life—and of pain.

As Emma sat in the darkened room beside her father, the past flowed into the present. Could it be nearly twenty years ago that he had read her first shyly adolescent poems and encouraged her? And after her mother died, how he had sustained her! How much she owed to him for not having forced upon her the conventional social role. With the Lazarus fortune for a dowry and her own striking charm, she could have married well. He had not sought to influence her.

Had he felt that her poetry, her need for expression left room for nothing else? If so, he had not understood all her need for expression.

Her zeal and her accomplishment might have been even greater had she been fulfilled as a woman, as a wife and mother. For this longing and identification was ever present in her poems. It is remarkable in how many of her poems the image of a woman, and especially of a mother, occurs. An intimation of this need came to her as she tended her father, and the impending loss made her aware, more keenly, of what she had missed in her life. But she was thirty-five, a mature woman—these thoughts were dashed out of her mind by her father's needs. . . .

Perhaps she had put obstacles in her own path; at any rate, they had long been there, and by now seemed impossible to dislodge. No matter how often she was told she was attractive, she never quite believed it. And quite possibly, she had set her standards too high at too early an age. She had been a precocious child, had gone forward to deeper wisdom, fuller understanding. She had met many young men, liked several of them—Tom Ward, for example—as friends and as companions. But none of them seemed to give her the kind of rapport, the empathy her spirit demanded. For better, for worse, she could not be satisfied with talking about dances or games; she preferred discussions of philosophy, of Greek and Latin poetry. She could talk with Emerson, the venerable sage of Concord, or with Dr. Gottheil, or with an editor like Philip Cowen. But if there were younger men about to match her, she had not yet, at 35, found them.

She hurried downstairs to call her older sister, Sarah. Father had definitely taken a turn for the worse; the family doctor must be summoned immediately.

In March, 1885, Moses Lazarus died. Though the end had been anticipated, it came as a tragic, numbing shock. After the funeral, Emma found life in the bereaved house on Tenth Street unbearable. She must get away.

Together with her sister Josephine, she mapped out a tour of the Continent. They would leave this house, with its agonized memories. For Emma believed sternly and joyously in life.

14

REKINDLED

🌷 Their itinerary was to include England again, and France, and the Low Countries—and perhaps Italy. For how long? They left that for the future. During this plan-making she recalled an interesting piece she had seen in the *American Hebrew*, about a writer of a Midrash —a biblical exegesis—"who hurled his satire at the head of a contemporary priest." What was the author's name? Schnabel, yes, that was it. She turned to Philip Cowen for confirmation. "Will you have the kindness to send me a copy of the *American Hebrew* containing Mr. Schnabel's version of the Midrash—I have mislaid my copy, and should be very much obliged if you would let me have another—" (The dashes at the end of a sentence, how like her impatience and eagerness, Cowen thought. "I am going abroad for an indefinite period, and I expect to sail for Liverpool on the 16th of May. If you have any communications to make, while I am away, my address will be care Messrs. Baring Brothers, Bishopgate St., London—"

If he had any communications to make—and she was going away for an indefinite period. . . . Of course he would want to remain in touch with her, and of course she knew it.

Then he smiled at her concluding paragraph. Let no one tell him that poets lived in ivory towers, and were unconcerned with the real world—and royalty payments! For she complained: "You have never rendered me any account of the sales of *Songs of a Semite*. Is it possible that there have been no pecuniary returns except such as cover the outlay?"

Emma and Josephine sailed in fine May weather. The

Atlantic crossing was pleasant, the beginning of their European tour auspicious. Philip Cowen kept in touch with Emma by correspondence. Sir Moses Montefiore, the British philanthropist, had died. The *American Hebrew* was planning a memorial issue to honor him. Would Miss Lazarus care to send in a poem, or a written tribute of some sort?

From Cambridge, Emma replied: "I am in receipt of your favor—and thank you for giving me the chance to contribute to your proposed Montefiore Memorial. I regret to say, however, that in the hurry and confusion of my present mode of life in traveling, I shall not be able to devote the requisite time and thought to such a work—Wishing you all success, and with thanks for your kind inquiries which find me in excellent health—"

Her health did seem improved. She and her sister had spent the summer at a country house in Yorkshire. It was good to wake up to the sight of trees, to green grass, to a landscape creamy with abundance. Emma felt newly refreshed and inspired. "The very air seems to rest one here," she exclaimed. She began a novel.

The first few chapters went speedily; then the work faltered and slowed to a standstill. Was her heart fully in the theme, or was it bodily weakness returning?

For, despite the relaxed atmosphere of the country house in Yorkshire, she was not feeling quite as well as she should. Sighing, she gave up the novel and turned her attention to her heap of unanswered letters. Into these answers went intimations of her unhappy state. "I have," she wrote, "neither ability, energy, nor purpose. It is impossible to do anything, so I am forced to set the novel aside for the present; whether to take it up again in the future remains to be seen."

Change of scene was an illusion, she knew. One's own spirit, the portable landscape, goes everywhere. Yet she would try another change of scene. . . . In the autumn, she went with her sister to Holland, and from there wrote, in a happier frame of mind: "We have been visiting The Hague—it completely fascinated me, and I feel stronger and more cheerful than I have for many a day."

From the Low Countries, she went on to France. "Paris," she wrote, "amazes me with its splendor and magnificence! All the ghosts of the Revolution are somehow laid. . . ." The autumn weather was invigorating; she walked everywhere, including miles through the art museums. . . .

Then Italy, to her poet's mind, the magical land "where Dante and where Petrarch trod!" She had translated those great Italian poets into English.

The reality was as beautiful as her dream. Again she kept a diary to store away her impressions: "Each tower, castle and village shining like a jewel; the olive, the fig, and at your feet the roses, growing in mid-December—"

Pisa, Florence, and finally, Rome, "wiping out all other places and impressions, and opening a whole new world of sensations. I am wild with the excitement of this tremendous place. I have been here a week, and have seen the Vatican and the Capitoline Museums, and the Sistine Chapel, and St. Peter's, besides the ruins on the streets and on the hills, and the graves of Shelley and Keats. It is all heart-breaking. I don't mean only those beautiful graves overgrown with acanthus and violets, but the mutilated arches and columns and dumb appealing fragments looming up in the glowing sunshine under the Roman blue sky."

The past loomed strong. "The far-away past, that seems so sad and strange and near. I am even out of humour with pictures; a bit of broken stone or a fragment of a bas-relief, or a Corinthian column standing out against this lapis-lazuli sky, or a tremendous arch, are the only things I can look at for the moment—except the Sistine Chapel, which is as gigantic as the rest, and forces itself upon you with equal might."

Spring comes early in Italy. With delight, she observed that in February "the almond-trees are in bloom, violets cover the grass, and oh! the divine, the celestial, the unheard-of beauty of it all!"

She felt keenly, opened her emotions. In her surged a strange duality of joy and pain. Was it the reluctant awareness of her illness forcing itself upon her exultant spirit? She took note of her own "strange mixture of longing and regret and delight. I have to exert all my strength not to lose myself in morbidness and depression."

A summer spent once more in the placid English countryside restored her somewhat. And she was pleased to see her article on William Morris at last in print. She hoped she had presented his ideas convincingly. When she had finished the manuscript, she sent him a copy to look over. The vigorous old gentleman had returned it promptly, commenting, "The quotations are just what I should have liked to see quoted, and express my present view as clearly as ever."

But how would the readers of the *Century* react to "A Day in Surrey with William Morris"? The article appeared in July of 1886, at the height of the furore over the Haymarket affair in Chicago. Labor leaders were thrown in jail; socialism became a swear-word. William Morris was a poet and artisan—he was also a socialist, and Emma had not tried to disguise the fact:

"Mr. Morris' extreme socialistic convictions are the subject of so much criticism at home, that a few words concerning them may not be amiss here. Rather would he see the whole framework of society shattered than a continuance of the actual conditions of the poor. 'I do not want art for a few, any more than education for a few or freedom for a few. No, rather than that art should live this poor, thin life among a few exceptional men, despising those beneath them for an igorance for which they themselves are responsible, for a brutality which they will not struggle with; rather than this, I would that the world should indeed *sweep away all art for a while*. . . . Rather than the wheat should rot in the miser's granary, I would that the earth had it, that it might yet have a chance to quicken in the dark.'

"The above paragraph from a lecture delivered by Mr. Morris before the Trades' Guild of Learning, gives the key to his socialistic creed, which he now makes it the main business of his life to promulgate. . . . No thwarted ambitions, no stunted capacities, no narrow, sordid aims have ranged him on the side of the disaffected, the agitator, the outcast.

"As poet, scholar, householder, and capitalist, he has everything to lose by the victory of that cause to which he has subordinated his whole life and genius. The fight is fierce and bitter; so thoroughly has it absorbed his energies, so filled and inspired and illumined is he with his aim, that it is only after leaving his presence we realize it is to this man's strong and delicate genius we owe the enchanting visions of *The Earthly Paradise,* and *Sigurd the Volsung,* the story of Jason, and *The Aeneid of Virgil.*"

There were no devastating repercussions from her article— at least none that reached across the Atlantic to disturb the serenity of the English countryside where she was now resting.

She was resting, and yet she still felt tired, so very tired. Such a heaviness seemed to be settling in all her limbs; she must shake it off!

Perhaps if she were to return to the places where she had been happy and energetic before?

So to Holland again, and to Paris in the autumn of 1886. Once the winter ended, she could go back to Italy. There the early spring, the fabulous blue of the Mediterranean sky, the golden Italian sunshine would restore her. Surely it would? Oh, would it not? She dared not face that possibility.

For her illness was now evident. It was no mere languor. It was pain, and it was pain, and it was present. Still, the doctors

were not yet able to diagnose the disease as cancer. But the
ailment was spreading; that much they knew. . . .

Emma pretended not to notice everyone's alarm and sympathy. She planned a springtime journey to Italy. If she were
not strong enough to go tomorrow—well, then next week . . .
then next month. . . .

She alternated between gaiety and despair. The image of
Heine haunted her. Heine, the poet, the Jew, an alien in Paris,
and on a sickbed. The indentification became intense. She
thought of Heine racked with pain, his body wasting away,
dragging himself up for one last look at beauty. His agonizing
final visit to the museum to see the classic statue of Venus.

Two years before, she had written a sonnet about that incident. How prophetic her words now seemed as she recalled
the lines she had written:

VENUS OF THE LOUVRE

Down the long hall she glistens like a star,
The foam-born mother of Love, transfixed to stone,
Yet none the less immortal, breathing on.
Time's brutal hand hath maimed but could not mar.
When first the enthralled enchantress from afar
Dazzled mine eyes, I saw her not alone,
Serenely poised on her world-worshipped throne,
As when she guided once her dove-drawn car,—
But at her feet a pale, death-stricken Jew,
Her life adorer, sobbed farewell to love.
Here Heine wept! Here still he weeps anew,
Nor ever shall his shadow lift or move,
While mourns one ardent heart, one poet-brain,
For vanished Hellas and Hebraic pain.

Now, gripped with pain herself, she too insisted upon seeing
the same "goddess without arms, who cannot help."

But her body must not conquer her mind! Back from the
exhausting visit, she determined anew that she would not be
defeated. The fire had flickered low, but she would keep the
embers glowing.

Fire needs air. Conscious of how far she was extending herself, triumphant in the strength of her will, she fought back against death. She would not allow the door to close, the blinds to be drawn!

So she could say without conceit, yet with full awareness of her condition, "I seem always to have one little window looking out into life."

The image pleased her, and when she was permitted to get up from bed and sit on the little balcony, she felt like weeping tears of joy and gratitude. She was going to live!

She began to speak of her disease as a thing of the past. She was allowed to take short drives. She could sit up and read; she could walk about the little balcony. "There is no such cure for pessimism as a severe illness," she told her friends. "The simplest pleasures become enough—to breathe the air and see the sun."

But her disease resumed its course. Talk of returning to Italy was finally given up. The question now became: how soon could she leave for America, for home? And she made her mind work harder than ever.

She had always loved music; now she reacted to it with all her soul. She thought she had never before realized to what depths of tragedy—yes, and to what heights of tragedy—the chords of Bach and Beethoven reached. Above unhappiness and sorrow, rose their high affirmation, their "yes!" to life.

She responded similarly to great painting. She planned a work on the "genius and personality" of Rembrandt, a probing, critical analysis, seeking out his relation to the people and the events of his period of history. A genius like Rembrandt walked in the world, was of the world. People must be made to see that artists were not a group apart; no, the painter and beholder, the poet and reader, the composer and listener were alike participants, together, in life. Otherwise how could any artist hope to communicate? How could his expression have any meaning, any scope? When she was still a very young woman, still groping for expression, she had written:

> Who seeks, shall find—
> Widening knowledge surely brings
> Vaster themes to him who sings.

Now, as her body lay racked with pain, her spirit was calm: she had been true to herself. She thought of an early poem she had written. . . .

It had been a sultry summer night, the full August moon shedding a glory of silver over the landscape. Emma walked in the radiance. In her poem she had recalled:

> . . . All the shapes by poet's brain
> Fashioned, live for me again,
> In this spiritual light,
> Less than day, yet more than night.
> What a world! a waking dream,
> All things other than they seem,
> Borrowing a finer grace,
> From yon golden globe in space.
> Who would marvel should he find
> In the copse or nigh the spring,
> Summer fairies gamboling
> Where the honey-bees do suck,
> Mab and Ariel and Puck?
> Ah! no modern mortal sees
> Creatures delicate as these.
> All the simple faith has gone
> Which their world was builded on.
> Now the moonbeams coldly glance
> On no gardens of romance.

But that had been only one aspect of the scene. Young and impressionable as she had been, no magic of moonlight could compare, even then, with the living, breathing human world. So her poem had continued:

> I am one
> Who would not restore that Past,
> Beauty will immortal last,
> Though the beautiful must die—
> This the ages verify. . . .

> . . .   .

I behold without regret,
Beauty in new forms recast,
Truth emerging from the vast,
Bright and orbed, like yonder sphere,
Making the obscure air clear.

She had envisioned the role of the true poet, the bold trumpeting singer—not the sighing troubadour twanging away at worn-out classic or romantic themes:

He shall be of bards the king,
Who, in worthy verse, shall sing
All the conquests of the hour,
Stealing no fictitious power
From the classic type outworn,
But his rhythmic line adorn
With the marvels of the real.
He the baseless feud shall heal
That estrangeth wide apart
Science from her sister Art.

Now many of the lines seemed immature to her, mechanical in their easy rhymes, their tick-tock rhythm; but the idea was still valid; she need not feel ashamed.

How much there was to write of in the real world! A lifetime as long as Methusaleh's would not be enough. . . .

She proceeded with her book on Rembrandt, despite the weakness of her body.

But it was now clear that no medicine, no palliative could stave off the tragic end. She could not remain in Paris. Yet the ocean voyage would be a great strain upon her; still she must go home. She was an American; she would end her days there.

On July 23, the day after her thirty-eighth birthday, she sailed for home. Emma arrived in New York on July 31 and was immediately taken to her sister's house on West Tenth Street.

Now the disease was easy to diagnose by its tortures: cancer. Her sister Josephine, writing the biographical preface to Emma's poems a year after her death, recalled these final months: "And now began her long agony, full of every kind of suffering, mental

and physical. Only her intellect seemed kindled anew, and none
but those who saw her during the last supreme ordeal can realize
that wonderful flash and fire of the spirit before its extinction.
Never did she appear so brilliant. Wasted to a shadow, and
between acute attacks of pain, she talked about art, poetry, the
scenes of travel, of which her brain was so full."

Articulate as ever, the observant writer always in command
of her creative powers, she even spoke of her own condition
with detachment and clarity. She spoke of everything, Josephine
noted, "with an eloquence for which even those who knew her
best were quite unprepared. Every faculty seemed sharpened
and every sense quickened."

It was the autumn, her beloved time of year, the fragrant and
fruitful harvest season. On the morning of November 19, she
died.

Two days later she was buried in the family plot at Cypress
Hills Cemetery. On Saturday, November 26, on the Jewish
Sabbath, she was eulogized in pulpits throughout the land.

The day was dedicated to her memory; to studies of her life
and work. The highest in the literary world bowed to honor
her. John Greenleaf Whittier said that "her people will mourn
the death of this woman, but they will not be alone. At her
grave the tears of the daughters of Jerusalem will mingle with
those of the Christians." George W. Cable, the Southern writer,
spoke for the conscience of many: "She was the worthy daughter
of a race to which the Christian world owes a larger debt of
gratitude, incurred from the days of Abraham until now, and
from which it should ask more forgiveness than to and from
any other people that ever trod the earth." Robert Browning
sent a message to the *American Hebrew,* associating himself
"with the admiration for the genius and love of the character
of my lamented friend." Harriet Beecher Stowe honored her
memory. Many other tributes came from preachers and poets,

from historians and critics, from the Secretary of State, from leaders of the Jewish community, from the editors of the most influential newspapers and magazines in the land. Whitman regretted that he had never met her: "She must have had a great, sweet, unusual nature."

15

"WOMAN WITH A TORCH"

🌼 The year following Emma's death, her poems were gathered together by her sisters, Mary and Annie. Josephine wrote a biographical preface, and the collected poems were issued in two volumes by H. O. Houghton and Company, Emma's original publishers.

The olive-green books included all the poems the sisters cared to preserve. They favored the earlier verses on classical and romantic themes.

Then the two volumes were left to gather dust. But some of her outstanding poems were included in the anthology her friend Edmund Clarence Stedman published in 1900.

After that, nothing but a desultory article or two about her until Morris U. Schappes re-introduced her to the public in 1944, with a selection from her poems and polemical pieces, and then, on the centennial of her birth, with an edition of her letters.

Why was she neglected for so long? Why, when she had so much to say to her own age and to our own, has she been forgotten?

Who is Emma Lazarus? Oh, yes, "give me your tired, your poor"—that poem on the Statue of Liberty; isn't her name engraven on the pedestal or somewhere? And that is just about the sum of it.

The misconceptions have been many . . . that she was an immigrant herself . . . a poorly paid social worker . . . a suffragette . . . even, not unexpectedly in these days of skin-deep, sin-deep psychologizing, that she had a "father complex." So

H. C. Jacobs in *The World of Emma Lazarus* insists that she was a thwarted spinster, a brooding, Brontë-esque character, secretly in love with her father and he incestuously with her. . . . This caused her to champion the Jews. . . .

There are reasons for the misunderstandings and the mysteries. Her diaries, which would have provided clues to her growth as an artist and as a human being, were never made public—except the fragments quoted in her sister Josephine's biographical preface to the poems.

The preface itself is plaintive, reticent: "One hesitates to lift the veil," Josephine wrote, "on so shrouded a life and spirit. . . ." She refers to Emma as a "hidden, withdrawn personality."

From Emma's work, from her letters, her life itself, we know that she was ardent and eager. Yet, for many, many years, the veiled figure in Josephine's biographical essay, the only study available, was all the world knew of Emma Lazarus.

Then, too, not all her family was in sympathy with her ideas. Her younger sister Annie became a convert to Catholicism, in the face of Emma's contention that "converted Jews are probably not only the most expensive of all marketable commodities, but also the most worthless after they are purchased." At any rate, she did not wish Emma to be remembered as a "Jewish poet."

No, Annie Lazarus Humphreys-Johnstone took a deep breath and exhaled a long-winded but plain-spoken regret that there was a "tendency on the part of some of Emma's public to overemphasize the Hebraic strain in her work, giving it thus a quality of sectarian propaganda which I greatly deplore, for I understood this to have been merely a phase in my sister's development, called forth by righteous indignation at the tragic happenings of those days. Then, unfortunately, owing to her untimely death, this was destined to be her final word."

This was straight wishful thinking on Annie's part. Of course it is tragic that Emma died when she was only thirty-eight, that she was cut off at the height of her creative powers. But had she been able to live out her life to the ripeness of age, her ideas would have remained; they were the body and soul of her belief and her art. She would never have exchanged her "perpetual lamp" of truth and justice for any lesser light.

Never. Emma had, as Walt Whitman realized, "a great, sweet, unusual nature." She was conscious of her triple role as an American, as a woman, as a Jew—and she was equally proud of all three.

One of the finest women poets our country has produced, she enriched the treasure-house of American democratic writing. She should be reclaimed and honored.

Her achievement is wider. For, although she never dared appear on a public platform, her words spoke directly to the consciences of Jew and non-Jew alike. Her "Jewish Idea" was the idea of humanity.

Many of her concepts are so current, so in the mainstream of today's thinking, that it is almost incredible that they were conceived sixty and seventy years ago—and by a woman reared in a sheltered, almost hothouse atmosphere. From it she lifted herself up by her own mental strength.

The spirit of the famous statue of "Liberty Enlightening the World" is the spirit of Emma Lazarus herself. And although it is ironic that she is remembered, for the most part, only as the author of this single poem, it is good that the words should be so widely known and loved. For this sonnet represents the climax, the crown of her beliefs. An entire philosophy of living is summed up in the fourteen brief lines.

Emma Lazarus gloried in her Americanness, her womanliness, her Jewishness—and America was the towering symbol of all three. For it was the New World—with a place for women to express themselves, to come forward from the back stair, from the chair in the corner, into the full range of human activity; with a place for Jews, for all refugees, to find the family warmth of a homeland, to be respected as Jewish Americans, Polish Americans, German, French, Swedish, Turkish, every nationality. A mingling of many peoples, Negro and white, a nation busy with the work of peace.

Therefore she can begin her poem:

> Not like the brazen giant of Greek fame,
> With conquering limbs astride from land to land; . . .

No. *Her* America was not warlike, did not impose brute force. It was a figure with the most formidable strength in the world: the strength of freedom. It is the America we love:

> Here at our sea-washed, sunset gates shall stand . . .

What a wonderful image of New York harbor!

> A mighty woman with a torch, whose flame
> Is the imprisoned lightning, and her name
> Mother of Exiles. . . .

Not war. Not victory. Not success, nor wealth. America is the land of *liberty*. And the female figure symbolizing the idea is not a goddess, not a queen, not a jeweled courtesan. No, the mighty woman with a torch is awesomely ordinary—majestic with commonplace experience: *Mother of Exiles.*

> From her beacon hand
> Glows world-wide welcome; her mild eyes command
> The air-bridged harbor that twin cities frame. . . .

The mother accepts all: not merely the superior child, the exceptional; she does not cradle the blonde, blue-eyed to the exclusion of the darker; she plays no favorites, sets no quotas, makes no restrictions, for her love is a mother's, her *welcome* is *world-wide*, her heart is lavish and never-emptying. Her gaze is not belligerent, nor fearful; her eyes are mild.

> "Keep, ancient lands, your storied pomp," cries she
> With silent lips. . . .

She utters no threats, no intimidations; she cries with silent lips, like a mother humming a lullaby, offering the breathing warmth and security of her quietly comforting presence.

> *"Give me your tired, your poor,*
> *Your huddled masses yearning to breathe free,*
> *The wretched refuse of your teaming shore.*
> *Send these, the homeless, tempest-tost to me."*

I love you as you are, my own, my all, my children of the world. The wet, the cold, the hungry, the cast-out, the denied, the spat-upon—all shall be warmed, clothed, fed, sanctified by love, by liberty's maternal embrace.

> *"I lift my lamp beside the golden door!"*

Be not afraid of the darkness; *I lift my lamp,* the lamp of liberty, the steady glow of love. Shadows disappear; the door is opened wide; light shines in, golden with future promise, with a new world of hope, with the fulfilment of peace and freedom. Here and now, the golden door of dream leading to deed, of freedom blazoning clear and bright, forever, for all.

AFTERWORD

Emma Lazarus and Jewish Identity*

It is pointed out by Henrietta Szold in *The Jewish Encyclopedia* that the Lazarus family, although "ostensibly Orthodox in belief," had not, by 1883, "participated in the activities of the Synagogue or of the Jewish community." And the Rev. Dr. Gustav Gottheil, in his eulogy at Temple Emanu-El after her death, records the following: "For some years before 1882, I had asked her aid in the work I had already at that time in hand, of issuing a hymn-book for Jewish worship. Her reply was, 'I will gladly assist you as far as I am able; but that will not be much. I shall always be loyal to my race, but I feel no religious fervor in my soul.' " When Dr. Gottheil's *Hymns and Anthems Adapted for Jewish Worship* appeared in 1887 there was an index to what Emma Lazarus meant by "as far as I am able." The volume contains her versification of Ecclesiastes, XII, and two of her translations from Moses Ben Ezra, together with much other work by Harriet Beecher Stowe, Whittier, Emerson, William Cullen Bryant, Longfellow, Robert Burns, and Harriet Martineau. Unless one insists on identifying Jewish consciousness with "religious fervor" one could not support the interpretation of the complete suddenness of the change; it is noteworthy that Dr. Gottheil himself, deploring her indifference to religion, praises her loyalty to Jewry.

On the positive side, the following evidence exists. In her book, Admetus (1871), there is the poem written in 1867, "In the Jewish Synagogue at Newport." Those who consider this poem "detached," "impersonal," or lacking in "kinship with these dead Jews" might do well to compare the treatment of the theme with the poem in the same volume, "In a Swedish Graveyard." The poem was immediately reprinted in *The Jewish Messenger* of May 5, 1871, and again on March 29, 1872. And Henry Samuel Morais, in *Eminent Israelites of the Nineteenth Century*, published in 1880, *before* the developments which are held responsible for the too sudden change wrote: "Her lines in 'The Jewish Synagogue at Newport' are full of pathos and religious sentiment."The poem is included within for the reader to make his own estimate. If one wants a clue to the difference between her consciousness of Judaism in 1867 and in 1882, one can examine in this connection her stricture on the last stanza of Longfellow's poem on the same theme. In one she thinks only of the Jews of the past; in the later one, of the Jews of the vital present.

But even when the subject was not specifically Jewish, and most of her poems of that period were not, sometimes her phrasing will reveal her, as in

---

*See also pages iv. to viii. of the Introduction.

the first two lines of "The Day of Dead Soldiers, May 30, 1869," written on the second Memorial Day:

Welcome, thou gray and fragrant *Sabbath-day.*
To deathless love and valor dedicate!

Then there is her *life-long* interest in Heine: her first translations of his poems appeared in 1867, her last article on him in December 1884, less than three years before her death. She was not only an excellent translator of this poet so difficult to translate well. Having translated "Donna Clara" she was also stimulated to write two "Imitations," "Don Pedrillo" and "Fra Pedro," in which she fulfills what she declares to have been Heine's original intention. Yet the translations and the imitations together were first published in *The Jewish Messenger* for February 18, 1876. Can one read the poem, with its last lines orotund with the pride in Jewry, without realizing that Heine and Emma Lazarus were sharing a common triumph and a common knowledge of the nature of persecution?

It is also commonly assumed that her interest in the medieval Spanish Hebrew poets, and her translations of their poems, date from the period after 1881-1882. But here the record to the contrary is unmistakable: translations by Emma Lazarus of poems of Gabirol are published in *The Jewish Messenger* for January 17 and January 31, 1879, while translations from Judah Halevy appear in the same periodical in the issues of January 24, February 7, February 14, and February 21, 1879. These translations, it is specified, are from the versions in German made by Dr. Michael Sachs and Prof. Abraham Geiger, but they are the ones later included in the 1889 edition of *The Poems of Emma Lazarus.* While it is true that she did not begin to study the Hebrew language, under the guidance of Mr. Louis Schnabel and/or others, until the later period, her enthusiasm for a Gabirol and a Halevy, perhaps stimulated by Heine, is of much earlier date.

The final consideration in tracing the progress of Emma Lazarus' growing interest in Jewishness to the point where a definite qualitative change is noticeable, is the date of *composition* of her impressive play, *The Dance to Death.* The family's biographical sketch, followed of course by most other writers, accepts as fact the theory that the work was written in 1882, as a reaction to the Russian pogroms. Contrary and apparently conclusive evidence is offered, however, by Mr. Philip Cowen, printer of *The American Hebrew* in Emma Lazarus' time. In *The American Hebrew* of July 5, 1929, in "Recollections of Emma Lazarus," he quotes a letter from Emma Lazarus herself, received by the editors of that magazine on May 25, 1882, in which she wrote: "A *few years* ago I wrote a play founded on an incident of medieval persecution of the Jews in Germany, which I think it would be highly desirable to publish now, in order to arouse sympathy and to emphasize the cruelty of the injustice done to our unhappy people. I write to ask if The American Hebrew Publishing Company will undertake to print it in pamphlet form..." (My emphasis–M.U.S.)

Morris U. Schappes
(1982)

INDEX

Bibliography

A major reference entry on Emma Lazarus 1849-1887 by Diane Lichtenstein, is in *Jewish Women in America, Vol. I,* pp. 806-809, Routledge, NY and London, 1997.

Jaffe-Gill, Ellen. *The Jewish Woman's Book of Wisdom,* Carol Publishing Group, 1998. (Contains selection of Emma Lazarus' poems in wisdom genre)

Janowitz, Anne. "Torch Songs. The Poetry, Politics and Identity of Emma Lazarus," *The Jewish Quarterly.* (London) Spring, 1996 43(1) pp. 37-41.

Klein, Emma. *Emma Lazarus: Poet of the Jewish People.* Arthur James Publisher, Berkhamsted, Herts. UK 1997.

Lichtenstein, D. "The Words and Worlds of Emma Lazarus," *Writing Their Nations: The Tradition of 19th Century American Jewish Women Writers,* Indiana University Press, 1992.

Vogel, D. "Emma Lazarus: A Source of Inspiration," *American History,* March/April, 1996. v. 31(1) pp. 16-20.

_____. "The American Zionism of Emma Lazarus," *Amit Magazine,* NY. Winter 1999, v. LXXI, No. 1, pp. 19-22.

Wolosky, Shira. "An American Jewish Typology/Emma Lazarus and the Figure of Christ," *Prooftexts,* May, 1996, Vol.2, pp. 113-25.

Young, Bette Roth. *Emma Lazarus in Her World/Life and Letters.* Foreword by Francine Klagsbrun. Jewish Publication Society, Philadelphia, 1995. (Contains an essential and extensive bibliography of Lazarus up to 1995)

_____. "Emma Lazarus and Her Jewish Problem," *American Jewish History,* December, 1996. (84)4, pp. 291-313.

Similar essay on this topic is in Klagsbrun Introduction to Young biography of Lazarus in 1995. (See Schappes Introduction and Afterword in this Merriam book for an opposing view)

Note: For readers interested in Jewish immigration to USA and New York City during E. Lazarus lifetime, see Chapter 2, *The Promised City* by Moses Rischin, Harvard University Press, 1962.

About the Author

Born Eve Moskowitz, Philadelphia, July 19, 1916. (Her parents had emigrated from Russia as children). Merriam died in New York City, August 11, 1992.

Eve Merriam attended the University of Pennsylvania graduating in 1937, when she enrolled at Columbia University. A teacher suggested at the time she might find work if she changed her surname, whereupon she chose Merriam from the Merriam-Webster Dictionary on her desk. Married four times, she was the mother of two sons by her second husband, Martin Michel.

As a poet, her first book was *Family Circle*, awarded a Yale Series of Younger Poets publication. Her writing career included over 50 books of poems for children, and two plays in verse, *The Inner City Mother Goose*, 1971, and in 1958, *The Double Bed from the Feminine Side*. (The former became a Broadway show). In 1976 she also wrote *The Club*, a play. Many of her works were reprinted internationally.

Her best known books were *Figleaf: The Business of Being in Fashion* (1960); *Mommies at Work* (1961); *After Nora Slammed the Door* (1964); *The Real Book of Franklin D. Roosevelt* (1952) and *Martin Luther King*, 1971. She also wrote a young people's edition, *The Voice of Liberty*, 1959, of this book (orig. *Woman with a Torch*).

Eve Merriam was an avowed feminist, and above all, a poet. During her lifetime she was known for her progressive political views, and was proud that she was born on July 19, the anniversary of the Seneca Falls Women's Rights Convention in 1848.